Marle
To

God. Un ot give up
the search. There is no
meaning to life without him.
Scars! Faulkner

His, Theirs and Ours

Scars!

His, Theirs and Ours

Gardner Hall

Scars!

His, Theirs and Ours

Published by Mount Bethel Publishing,
P.O. Box 123, Port Murray, NJ 07865,
www.MountBethelPublishing.com

ISBN: 978-0-9850059-4-8
Library of Congress Control Number: 2016914550

Cover Design: Kirby Davis

Printed in the United States of America

Dedication

To my wife, Beverly

Contents

Part 1

Their Scars

Chapter 1

Scars Talk!

"Blows that wound cleanse away evil; strokes make clean the innermost parts" (Proverbs 20:30).

Texts: Hebrews 11:32-40; Matthew 10:17-23; 1 Peter 4:12-16

The large muscular African man who worked at the Leticia Ranch in the Matobo Hills of Zimbabwe was the talk of all the teenage boys who camped there. His six-foot-four-inch frame towered not only over his peers from the isiNdebele tribe, but also over those of British descent who still controlled the country in the 1950's. The boys oohed and aahed when he effortlessly picked up half of a fifty-five gallon steel barrel full of mealie meal, a staple food in that part of Southern Africa. But what most grabbed their attention were the scars that covered his entire body, the reminders of a battle with a leopard. The scars were a kind of victor's trophy that declared to all, "I killed a leopard with my bare hands!"

When I asked my friend, Paddy Kendall-Ball, about his experiences in Southern Africa in the 1950's, the exploits of

the scar-covered African were among his most vivid memories.
The scars had an impact!

Charles Woods was not your stereotypical handsome
politician. His face was horribly scarred and disfigured. He
had no ears. His eyelids and nose were constructed by plastic
surgeons. I remember a playground joke I heard at F.D.
McArthur Elementary School in Birmingham, Alabama
in the 1960's about his speeches beginning with the words,
"Friends, Alabamians, Countrymen, lend me your ears."

Walt Guthrie, who was a political cartoonist for the
Birmingham Herald for twenty years, recalled children's
jokes about Woods.[1] He described Woods' appearance "as a
monster. In the crude, simplistic, purely physical way that
monsters exist to sheltered children."

And yet, in spite of his frightful appearance, Woods became
a highly respected citizen of Alabama and moderately
successful politician. He took on George Wallace in a race
for the Democratic nomination for governor in 1970 and
finished third. In 1974 he initially won the majority of votes
for Lieutenant Governor in Alabama before eventually losing
in a runoff to Jere Beasley.[2] After moving to Nevada, he
made a respectable run for the Senate in 1992 against Harry
Reid.

In Woods' case, his disfiguring scars were probably his
greatest political asset because they proclaimed to the whole
world, "I am a hero." He received them in World War 2

as a pilot transporting aviation fuel over the Himalaya Mountains to China. A pilot Woods was training made a mistake on takeoff resulting in a horrific crash that killed all onboard except for Woods who was dreadfully burned. He was transferred barely alive to Valley Forge General Hospital in Pennsylvania where he became a special case for the Nobel Prize winning Doctor Joseph Murray, who featured Woods in his autobiography, *Surgery Of The Soul: Reflections on a Curious Career.*[3] After being given the skin of a dead soldier and going through 24 operations, many with very little anesthesia, doctors released Woods back into the world, where he became a successful businessman in Dothan, Alabama.

Woods' scars talked! They almost talked him into the Lieutenant Governor's seat in Alabama and earned him widespread respect before his death in 2003.

Our Scars Talk

We all have scars. Each one tells a story. A scar on my forehead says that as a toddler I fell and busted my head! A scar on my finger reminds me that I should have been more careful as a teenager with a knife when I was trying to work with antenna wire for my ham radio. And, there's that exclamation mark on my abdomen from surgery on my appendix in the days before laparoscopic surgery.

Perhaps even more telling than our physical scars are our emotional ones, the ones that remind us of our thoughtless words, mistakes with our children and other painful sins that have affected us in the past. Each one has a lesson for us if we are listening.

Scars in the Bible

Violence against God's followers with its resulting scars is found all through the Bible. Many of God's children in Jewish history…

> … were tortured, refusing to accept release, so that they might rise again to a better life. Others suffered mocking and flogging, and even chains and imprisonment. They were stoned, they were sawn in two, they were killed with the sword. They went about in skins of sheep and goats, destitute, afflicted, mistreated— of whom the world was not worthy—wandering about in deserts and mountains, and in dens and caves of the earth. (Hebrews 11:36-39)

Some of these references bring distinct Biblical events to mind: Joseph (Gen. 29:30), Micaiah (1 Kings 22:44), Elisha (2 Kings 2:23), Jeremiah (20:2; 37:15), etc. Others seem to refer to events in books such as the Maccabees. Dedicated worship of Jehovah in the days before Christ often brought on vicious reactions.

Life was just as brutal for the apostles, prophets, witnesses and other believers in Jesus Christ in the first century. Collectively they suffered thousands, probably even tens of thousands of blows to their bodies along with other unspeakable acts of torture and abuse that left signs of mutilation all over their bodies.

Jesus tried to prepare his followers for the savage response of his enemies. Christianity was destined to be a religion of violence—not a promoter, but a receiver of it.

> Beware of men, for they will deliver you over to courts and flog you in their synagogues, and you will be dragged before governors and kings for my sake, to bear witness before them and the Gentiles…
>
> Brother will deliver brother over to death, and the father his child, and children will rise against parents and have them put to death, and you will be hated by all for my name's sake. But the one who endures to the end will be saved. (Matthew 10:17, 18, 21 22)

As they were receiving their vicious blows, the apostles prepared those who believed through their teaching to receive similar treatment.

> Beloved, do not be surprised at the fiery trial when it comes upon you to test you, as though something strange were happening to you.
>
> But rejoice insofar as you share Christ's sufferings, that you may also rejoice and be glad when his glory is revealed.
>
> If you are insulted for the name of Christ, you are blessed, because the Spirit of glory and of God rests upon you.

But let none of you suffer as a murderer or a thief or an evildoer or as a meddler. Yet if anyone suffers as a Christian, let him not be ashamed, but let him glorify God in that name. (1 Peter 4:12-16)

Scars as Powerful Symbols

All wars leave their scarred veterans. These become symbols for their cause. Jalynn Olsen Padilla wrote of the effect that Union veterans who were amputees had on the psyche of America after the Civil War.

> Union amputees quickly occupied a prominent position in postwar culture and society. Popular periodicals of the late nineteenth century frequently featured Civil War amputees in illustrations, sentimental stories, poetry and political narratives. For decades after the war's end, Americans' image of the Civil War veteran often included an empty sleeve or pant leg. The veterans' disabilities came to symbolize sacrifices made during the war effort.[4]

In a similar way, the wounds and scars of early Christians became a symbol of their unwavering faith. Vance Havner pointed out that at the Nicene Council in the 4th century A.D., of the 318 delegates attending, "fewer than 12 had not lost an eye or lost a hand or did not limp on a leg lamed by torture for their Christian faith."[5] Their scars were a part of a three-hundred-year legacy of being on the receiving end of merciless torture.

It was the will of God that his witnesses and early followers receive every angry blow and that every wound leave its mark. Why? Because scars are powerful witnesses, speaking more powerfully than words ever can. And what are the scars telling us? That is the message of the rest of the book.

Questions for reflection:

1. How have wounds cleansed away evil in your own life? How have they given you a better perspective about what life is all about?

2. Can you think of any "heroic" scars that others have?

3. Do you have some physical scars that remind of you of events in your life, both pleasant and not so pleasant? Discuss.

4. Read Hebrews 11:26-29. Discuss some of the Old Testament characters that would fit some of the specific descriptions in these verses? Some will be easier to identify than others. For example, no one mentioned in the Old Testament was "sawn asunder" but according to Jewish tradition, that is how Isaiah died.

5. If you were told that your faith would bring on the hatred of those you loved and even bring violence into your life, would you abandon it? If you give yourself completely over to God, will you be ridiculed? Is there a chance that one day you might have to even suffer imprisonment or physical punishment for your faith?

6. When God created the world, he knew there would be wounds and scars. Why? Would love exist if there were no wounds and scars?

Chapter 2

Their Scars

Paul and the Apostles

"Five times I received at the hands of the Jews the forty lashes less one. Three times I was beaten with rods. Once I was stoned" (2 Corinthians 11:24, 25).

Texts – 2 Corinthians 11:23-29; Acts 14:19, 20; 2 Corinthians 6:4-10

P aul's skin must have been a mass of scar tissue. You can do the math from 2 Corinthians 11:24—five times 39 lashes equals 195 stripes. Since the Law of Moses limited the number of lashes to forty (Deut. 25:3), the Jews traditionally gave 39 to make sure that they did not surpass the limitations of the law.

Adam Clarke quoted the Mishnah to describe physical punishment meted out by ancient Jews. The Mishnah is a

Jewish commentary on the Law of Moses edited about two hundred years after Christ. Its purpose was to sum up oral Jewish teachings that were disappearing after the destruction of Jerusalem.

> The two hands of the criminal are bound to a post, and then the servant of the synagogue either pulls or tears off his clothes till he leaves his breast and shoulders bare. A stone or block is placed behind him on which the servant stands; he holds in his hands a scourge made of leather, divided into four tails. He who scourges lays one third on the criminal's breast, another third on his right shoulder, and another on his left. The man who receives the punishment is neither sitting nor standing, but all the while stooping; and the man smites with all his strength, with one hand.[6]

Albert Barnes believes that the majority of Paul's 195 stripes would have been applied in the synagogues[7] as Jesus predicted in Matthew 10:17. Talk about church discipline! Paul knew all about beatings in the synagogues because he participated in them before becoming a Christian (Acts 22:19).

"Beaten Three Times with Rods"

This was a common punishment of cruel Roman authorities, especially the magistrates who judged affairs among Roman citizens.[8] They weren't concerned with niceties such as limiting the number of blows to 39. There are numerous references in Roman plays and literary works to the rods that the Romans used to beat others.[9] They were made of elms, birch, oak, ash, willow, vines and even occasionally of iron and lead.

We have details about one of these three beatings with rods in Acts 16:22, 23. Verses 22 and 23 describe what happened to Paul after being dragged to the magistrates for having healed a demon-possessed fortuneteller.

The crowd joined in attacking them, and the magistrates tore the garments off them and gave orders to beat them with rods. And when they had inflicted many blows upon them, they threw them into prison, ordering the jailer to keep them safely.

There were several types of beatings applied by the enforcers for the Roman magistrates ranging from "light corrective beating" given to free citizens with a military staff to a much harsher beating given to slaves and other less desirables.[10] The description of Paul and Silas's beating indicates they received the worst type. They were stripped of their clothing, received many blows and required a later washing of the wounds before their predawn baptism of the jailor (verse 33).

"Once I Was Stoned"

Acts 14 describes Paul's stoning in a brief and detached way.

But Jews came from Antioch and Iconium, and having persuaded the crowds, they stoned Paul and dragged him out of the city, supposing that he was dead. But when the disciples gathered about him, he rose up and entered the

city, and on the next day he went on with Barnabas to
Derbe. (vss. 19, 20)

There are no details about the thudding of the rocks against
Paul's body, the cracking bones, the spurting blood or the
moans that eventually died away, making the mob think that
he was dead.

It isn't difficult to imagine the horror and concern of the
newly formed little band of Christians coming out from
hiding after the mob moved away and furtively approaching
Paul's apparently lifeless body.

"He's still alive!" one would have exclaimed. Others would
have gathered around Paul's crumpled body trying to revive
their teacher while at the same dragging him to a hiding place
in case the mob returned.

Stoning would have been nothing new to Paul since, as in the
case of receiving beatings, he had once been on the giving end
of this barbaric act. He participated in the stoning of the first
martyr, Stephen (Acts 7:68).

Though the great majority of Paul's scars would have been on
his back, certainly some of the stones and rods would have
hit him on other parts of his body, including his face. It is
not difficult to imagine that he would have become an object
of curiosity to those who saw his face and especially his body.
"Whatever happened to him?" There's no wonder that when
Claudius Lysias, the Roman commander of Jerusalem, saw

Paul, he thought he was a terrorist (Acts 21:38). Perhaps his scarred appearance contributed to the accusation of some of his detractors that his bodily presence was weak (2 Cor. 10:10).

Paul's scars were so well known to others that he had no shame in referring to them in texts like Galatians 6:16 where he pled with those who were harming his work, "From now on let no one cause me trouble, for I bear on my body the marks of Jesus." Paul refers here to scars he had relatively early in his ministry. Even Paul's descriptions of his scars and other travails in preaching in 2 Corinthians chapter 11, were probably written towards the middle of his life. He still had many beatings and privations left to suffer! Though the book of Acts gives a summary of Paul's travels, 2 Corinthians chapter 11 indicates that it doesn't include a great number of details about them.

Their Scars – The Apostles

> …And when they had called in the apostles, they beat them and charged them not to speak in the name of Jesus, and let them go. Then they left the presence of the council, rejoicing that they were counted worthy to suffer dishonor for the name. (Acts 5:40,41)

As in the case of Paul's beatings by the Jews, each of the twelve here would have received the 39 lashes, possibly distributed between the two shoulders and the back. What is most astounding is how they responded to their thrashing. J.W. McGarvey says,

The statement that when they were released they went away
'rejoicing that they were counted worthy to suffer dishonor
for the name,' would be impossible, were it not written in a
book such as this, and written of men such as these.[11]

The beatings in Acts 5 were just the beginning of a life of
carnage for all twelve. Though there are few details in other
parts of the scripture about specific beatings they received,
they are implied throughout the New Testament and early
Christian history. James the brother of John and Peter would
have certainly received beatings at the hands of Herod's
henchmen while in custody before the execution of the
former and miraculous escape of the latter (Acts 12).

There are uninspired accounts of the lives of the 12 apostles
with varying degrees or reliability that indicate lives of great
suffering, including the following:

- Paul and Peter were probably martyred in Rome.

- Andrew probably preached in what is known now as
Russia before being martyred in Greece.

- There is a tradition that Thomas preached in India.

- Philip preached in North Africa where he converted
the wife of a proconsul and was therefore put to death.

- John died a natural death after his exile to the Island
of Patmos.

While some of these traditions may contain germs of truth, much more valuable is Paul's inspired and graphic description of the lives of the apostles including himself in 2 Corinthians 6:4-10.

> ...but as servants of God we commend ourselves in every way: by great endurance, in afflictions, hardships, calamities, beatings, imprisonments, riots, labors, sleepless nights, hunger; by purity, knowledge, patience, kindness, the Holy Spirit, genuine love; by truthful speech, and the power of God; with the weapons of righteousness for the right hand and for the left; through honor and dishonor, through slander and praise. We are treated as impostors, and yet are true; as unknown, and yet well known; as dying, and behold, we live; as punished, and yet not killed; as sorrowful, yet always rejoicing; as poor, yet making many rich; as having nothing, yet possessing everything.

Not only does Paul mention the persecution, but also the blessings enjoyed from their lives of privation: honor, praise, truth, life, rejoicing, enrichment of others and possession of everything. What a combination of anguish and joy! Talk about paradoxical lives! Why should we wonder that the testimony of these men turned the Roman world upside down? (Acts 17:6) Wherever they went, thousands of collective scars backed up their testimony.

Questions for reflection

1. Those who beat Paul obviously thought that abusing him would discourage him and hinder his efforts. The abuse obviously had the opposite effect. Why?

2. How do you think Paul's scars affected those who listened to him in a positive way? In a negative way? What type of people would it have affected in a positive way? What type of people would it have affected in a negative way? How does considering Paul's scars affect you?

3. In Acts 16:3, Paul wanted to take a young man named Timothy with him on his travels. How do you think Timothy's mother would have felt about her son accompanying a man who had been beaten and stoned for his faith? How would you feel as a parent if someone like Paul wanted your child to travel with him?

4. Why do you think the apostles were able to rejoice after being beaten? Who is someone or a cause for which you would feel honored to suffer?

5. What effect do you think that the apostles' rejoicing after being beaten would have on those who beat them? On those who observed? On those who sympathized with the apostles? Should their rejoicing in suffering have any less effect on us today because almost 2000 years have passed?

6. In the list of contrasts in the lives of the apostles, Paul mentioned, "as sorrowful, yet always rejoicing." What would be some things that would have made them sorrowful? What would be some things that would have made them rejoice? Which would most dominate their lives, sorrow or rejoicing?

Chapter 3

What Do the Apostles' Scars Say?

"I'm Telling the Truth!"

"Truthful lips endure forever, but a lying tongue is but for a moment" (Proverbs 12:19).

Texts - 1 Corinthians 15:3-8; Revelation 12:10,11; 2 Corinthians 4:7-15

Childhood memory - I would have been a second grader when I was playing in the bathroom with little boats in the tub. I heard my mother's voice from another part of the house saying, "Gardner, Where are you?"

That voice meant a chore—either cleaning up my room or something else. I hoped that if I ignored it, it would go away and I could continue to play with my boats. But, the voice was persistent, moving closer and closer to the den, then to the adjoining bedroom, "Gardner I know you're here somewhere." Finally it stopped by the bathroom door where I was listening as quiet as a mouse. "Gardner are you in there?"

"There's nobody in here," I found myself saying.

There was laughter and then my mother said, "There has to be somebody in there to say, 'there's nobody in here!'"

I couldn't refute that logic. I knew I was caught!

What was my motive for lying? Avoidance of work. That is a common motive for lying among many today.

Motives for Lying

Dr. Alex Lickerman states in an article in *Psychology Today* that in general we lie to protect ourselves in five areas:[12]

1. Ourselves personally – "to avoid suffering painful consequences, shame, embarrassment, or conflict."

2. Our interests

3. Our image

4. Our resources

5. Others

The first motive mentioned by Dr. Lickerman, "avoidance of suffering painful consequences, shame, embarrassment or conflict," describes precisely what the apostles and other witnesses received for stating that they saw the miracles of Jesus and his living body after his death and resurrection. Generally speaking, no one except an isolated megalomaniac would lie knowing that the lie would bring on unspeakable torture and pain. Therefore, when the twelve apostles plus around five hundred other witnesses (1 Cor. 15:6) unwaveringly claimed to have seen with their own eyes a dead man, Jesus, alive again, they must have been telling the truth! They knew that such an extraordinary and farfetched claim would bring on brutal agony and death and it did! To say that all were lying about what they saw with their own eyes so that they would suffer horribly is to overlook everything we know about human nature.

Historian Michael Licona states it this way in his book *The Resurrection of Jesus: A New Historiographical Approach*:

> After Jesus' death, the disciples endured persecution, and a number of them experienced martyrdom. The strength of their conviction indicates that they were not just claiming Jesus had appeared to them after rising from the dead. They really believed it. They willingly endangered themselves by publicly proclaiming the risen Christ.[13]

Their Scars Speak!

It's as if the thousands of collective scars on the backs of the apostles and other witnesses had lips to talk and were talking to us down through the centuries saying, "I'm telling the truth!" Every scar producing blow that was received on the backs and other body parts of these determined eyewitnesses added another layer of credibility to their testimony.

While we sometimes struggle with doubts, such was never the case with the apostles and other eyewitnesses. Not only were they driven to accept their scars, but also to travel to all corners of the known world with their message. How could they be so certain that they would willingly submit to grievous abuse? Because they actually saw what they said they saw!

Besides the beatings, mentioned earlier, Paul describes in 2 Corinthians 11 other hardships he suffered because of his testimony,

> Three times I was shipwrecked; a night and a day I was adrift at sea; on frequent journeys, in danger from rivers, danger from robbers, danger from my own people, danger from Gentiles, danger in the city, danger in the wilderness, danger at sea, danger from false brothers; in toil and hardship, through many a sleepless night, in hunger and thirst, often without food, in cold and exposure. (2 Corinthians 11:25-27)

Roughly multiply what Paul went through by twelve (actually more if you take into consideration other witnesses) and you get an idea of the single-minded determination of early Christian martyrs to get their message out with absolutely no regard for the nasty consequences. And someone wants to say that they were lying? Can't we see why the early message of Christ began to overpower the Roman Empire in the first century with no armies but humble laborers, no weapons but an overwhelming love and no complex philosophy but rather the simple message about a risen Savior? Behind it all were the witnesses to the miracles and resurrection of a humble carpenter. Did they have any doubts about what they had seen? They had none! Their lack of doubt should be a remedy for ours.

The translated words "witness" and "martyr" come from the same word in the New Testament. The martyrs (witnesses) were of great importance in the book of Revelation. (Rev. 12:11) Satan's battle against them and their eventual triumph is one of the key themes of the book. Chapter 12 relates the victory over Satan and verse 11 gives the two key elements of that victory. "And they have conquered him by the blood of the Lamb and by the word of their testimony, for they loved not their lives even unto death." It is remarkable that the testimony of the witnesses is almost placed on par with the blood of Christ as reasons for Satan's defeat. And what backed up their testimony so powerfully? The fact that even beatings and death did nothing to deter them! "They loved not their lives even unto death!" (Rev. 12:11). That fact explains the power of that testimony and why it has "turned the world upside down" (Acts 17:6).

What Do the Apostles' Scars Say? "I Love You"

"So death is at work in us, but life in you" (2 Cor. 4:12).

There is no love that is closer to God's love than a mother's love! It all begins with the pain of childbirth. A woman allows her body to go through shattering pain, but it's all worth it to bring the object of her love into this world. Love is the primary emotion that makes the pain of childbirth tolerable.

A mother's suffering for her children then continues through their childhood and teenage years. I know single mothers who have come to this country from Latin America whose whole lives are dedicated to providing an education and a better life for their children. No work is too demeaning for them, no hour too early to get up in the morning, no privation too much if their children need their time. It's all about their kids.

Paul compared his suffering for the Galatians to a mother's suffering for her children—"My little children, for whom I am again in the anguish of childbirth until Christ is formed in you!" (4:15).

Like a mother, Paul was willing to undergo any hardship and torture to help those struggling people he saw come to Christ. God gave Paul the privilege of discussing this in detail in 2 Corinthians 4 in a passage that is similar to 2 Corinthians 6 analyzed in the last chapter. He starts in verse

7 by making a contrast between the apostles, "jars of clay" and the power of God, "But we have this treasure in jars of clay, to show that the surpassing power belongs to God and not to us."

The first part of the following phrases in verses eight and nine has a description of what happened to the apostles as "jars of clay." The second part of the phrase describes what the power of God did for them in spite of their human weaknesses.

> We are afflicted in every way, but not crushed; perplexed, but not driven to despair; persecuted, but not forsaken; struck down, but not destroyed; always carrying in the body the death of Jesus, so that the life of Jesus may also be manifested in our bodies. For we who live are always being given over to death for Jesus' sake, so that the life of Jesus also may be manifested in our mortal flesh. So death is at work in us, but life in you.

"Death is at work in us, but life in you." The scars and sufferings of the apostles worked to give life to the Corinthians, by helping them believe.

After mentioning the fact that his faith compelled him to speak, Paul summed up the benefit that would come from his suffering and that of other apostles in verse 15, "For it is all for your sake, so that as grace extends to more and more people it may increase thanksgiving, to the glory of God."

The expression, "for your sake" also occurs in Colossians 1:24,

> Now I rejoice in my sufferings *for your sake*, and in my
> flesh I am filling up what is lacking in Christ's afflictions
> for the sake of his body, that is, the church...

Paul's sufferings and those of the other apostles were for the
sake of those early believers they knew, and for ours as well!

The second part of the Colossians 1:24 has caused some
head scratching among Bible students. How could there
be anything lacking in Christ's afflictions and His perfect
sacrifice? Certainly nothing is lacking in Christ's perfect
atoning sacrifice. However, God wanted much more suffering
than what Christ went through on the cross to back up
the testimony regarding Christ's miracles and especially his
resurrection. That's where the suffering of Paul and the other's
came in. To sum up by using some "doctrinal terms," what
was lacking was not atoning suffering but evidential suffering.

Just before his death, when writing Timothy Paul summed up
his love motive. "Therefore I endure everything for the sake
of the elect, that they also may obtain the salvation that is in
Christ Jesus with eternal glory" (2 Tim. 2:10).

The knowledge that their scars would help others and glorify
God must have been a factor in their pain tolerance level.
Each blow gave them satisfaction, knowing that it linked
them to their Lord and would ultimately help those they
loved to believe in the triumph of his cause.

Our primary thanks for the lives of hope we have as Christians goes to Jesus Christ and to the Father who sent Him. They made everything possible! However, it is impossible to think of the beaten, abused, tortured men who gladly gave their bodies over to be ripped and sliced to help us believe their stunning testimony, without being overwhelmed with gratitude for them as well.

Questions for reflection

1. What most tempted you to lie as a child? Which of the five reasons listed by Alex Lickerman tempts you most to lie now?

2. What are some of the most outlandish claims you have heard people make in places like grocery store tabloids or shock TV? (Think things like UFO's, seeing Elvis alive, etc.) Why do people make such claims? What is the difference between such outlandish claims and the claims of the apostles and other witnesses to have seen Jesus alive after his death?

3. When Jesus told the apostles they would be his witnesses (Acts 1:8), he was practically telling them that they would die for him. How would you feel if Jesus told you, "You will die for me?" Honored? Frightened? Sobered? How would that affect your prayer life?

4. Why do you think martyrs (witnesses) are so important in the book of Revelation? Are they still important to us today 2000 years later?

5. Who do you love in this world more than anyone else? What are some things you would be willing to go through for that person? Would you be willing to go through beatings and torture for that person?

6. Do you think the apostles and other witnesses might have thought about some specific people or congregations in mind that they were helping as they received their torture? When do you think it might have occurred to them that their sufferings helped others?

7. Think about Colossians 1:24. Can you see how Paul's sufferings might have filled up what was lacking in Christ's afflictions? Can our own scars in a sense fill in a very small way the story of Christ? (Think of what Christian slaves were to do according to Titus 2:10.)

Chapter 4

His Scars

Take Them Personally!

"But he was pierced for our transgressions; he was crushed for our iniquities; upon him was the chastisement that brought us peace, and with his wounds we are healed" (Isaiah 53:5).

Texts: Isaiah 53:1-12; Matthew 27:26-31; John 19:1-3, Galatians 2:20

The enemies of Jesus tried to hurt him spiritually for three years. What satisfaction it would have brought them if he had lashed out in a sinful response to their provocations! When they realized they would be unsuccessful in harming his spirit, their last recourse was to wound, torture and then kill his body. Little did they know that in doing so, they were kindling a fire that would cover the whole world. It was part of the plan of the Creator of the universe to instill within his creatures a sense of his love for them. The wounds and scars of the Son of God were an integral part of his plan! Christ's followers who have learned how to suffer have learned from the Master.

The Beatings

Perhaps the most graphic scene in the movie, the *Passion of Christ,* was the beating of Jesus by the Romans. Though director Mel Gibson exaggerated violence in several scenes,[14] the scourging scene accurately depicted the brutality of the actual event.

Physical abuse was a part of the process of the trial of Jesus long before he was "officially" beaten. The Jewish leaders started the process. Luke says,

> Now the men who were holding Jesus in custody were mocking him as they beat him. They also blindfolded him and kept asking him, "Prophesy! Who is it that struck you? (Luke 22:63.64)

The Roman soldiers continued this inhumane ridicule when the Jews handed Jesus over to them (Luke 23:1). They constantly pummeled him until the time came for the official beatings.

A comparison of John's crucifixion account with Matthew and Mark's seems to indicate that Jesus endured this brutal "official" lashing at least twice. John 19:1 says that Jesus was flogged before his sentencing to be crucified. Perhaps this was an effort on Pilate's part to evoke some sympathy from the Jews and therefore assuage their desire to crucify Jesus. That didn't work. Then Matthew and Luke indicate that he was also scourged after his sentencing (Matthew 27:26; Mark 15:15).

According to David McClister, "scourging, called verberatio by the Romans, was possibly the worst kind of flogging administered by ancient courts."[15] The victims often died. McClister pointed out that the Roman whip had "several (at least three) thongs or strands, each perhaps as much as three feet long, and the strands were weighted with lead balls or pieces of bone. This instrument was designed to lacerate. The weighted thongs struck the skin so violently that it broke open." He then quotes the ancient historian Eusebius regarding a scene of scourging. "The bystanders were struck with amazement when they saw them lacerated with scourges even to the innermost veins and arteries, so that the hidden inward parts of the body, both their bowels and their members, were exposed to view."[16] (*Ecclesiastical History*, Book 4, chap. 15).

Several suffering servant prophesies about Jesus from Isaiah seem to indicate some other startling facts about this process of beating, if they can be applied directly to the trial and crucifixion of Jesus as seems likely.

- "I gave my back to those who strike, and my cheeks to those who pull out the beard; I hid not my face from disgrace and spitting" (Isaiah 50:6). The emphasis of this

passage is the complete willingness of the suffering servant,
Jesus Christ, to give himself to his torturers! Though the four
gospels don't specifically mention the painful pulling out of
the Jesus' beard referenced in Isaiah, that is exactly the kind
of crude abuse to which he willingly submitted just before
his final sacrifice.

- "As many were astonished at you—his appearance
was so marred, beyond human semblance, and his form
beyond that of the children of mankind"(Isaiah 52:14).
Roman flogging was a disfiguring experience!

The Cross

Christians try to grasp the events at the cross and the
resurrection of Christ more than any other events in the
history of the world. Countless books and articles have tried
to get a handle on the medical aspects of Christ's death on the
cross and its spiritual implications.

What about the scars left by crucifixion? There is no
consensus on exactly where the nails would have gone into
the hands, although a good case can be made for the wrists,
"between the carpals and the radials."[17]

The discovery of the bones of a crucified Jewish man named
Yehohanan in a bone box (ossuary) from the first century has
given some answers about where the nails would probably
have been placed in the feet. [18] The discoverer, Vassilios
Tzaferis, wrote in *Biblical Archeology Review* that "a nail held

his heel bones together. The nail was about 7 inches (17–18 cm) long." Evidently most nails used to crucify victims were reused, but Yehohanan's nail had become bent by a knot in the wood, and thus was left in the wood with his bone attached.

What kind of scar would the wound in Jesus' side leave? Though there is no hard consensus, the fact that blood and water flowed from the wound indicates to some that the sac around the heart would have been pierced.[19] One thing is sure, there was a large wound in the side of Jesus and Jesus made reference to it to Thomas in John 20:21, implying that it was large enough for Thomas's hand to be inserted.

If the scars of men speak loudly to us, Immanuel's scars should be deafening. They are if we are listening. What do they tell us?

"I Love You – I Mean You!"

"Greater love has no one than this, that someone lay down his life for his friends" (Jn. 15:3).

With over seven billion people on the planet, it's hard for any one of them to feel very important.

"I'm just one of seven billion. Why am I important? Why would anyone care about me?"

The scars of Jesus say, "You are important." The scars of Jesus say, "I care."

If life continues until the year 4000, what will it be like then? Would anything we do now affect the way life would be in 4000? The apostles would have had little comprehension that their scar-supported testimony would still be changing millions of lives two thousand years in the future. I'm sure that life in the 21st Century would blow their minds and especially the fact that their testimony still has such an impact. Though I am extremely thankful for the scars of the apostles, and though they contribute greatly to my faith, they aren't my personal saviors. When they suffered, they could scarcely understand that someone like me might ever exist.

However, before Jesus came to earth, existing in the form of God (Phil. 2:5), he knew the scope of the blessings that would come from his wounds, his scars and his death. Now, he takes a personal interest in me, in my wounds, in my scars and in my battles. He knows that his suffering was for me and that his blood still cleanses me of my sin. "But if we walk in the light, as he is in the light, we have fellowship with one another, and the blood of Jesus his Son cleanses us from all sin" (1 Jn 1:7).

Personal Implications

I often think about Christ's death on the cross and his scars as being for the benefit of the great mass of mankind. Yes, his death was for all men (2 Cor. 5:15; 1 Tim. 2:4,5; Heb. 2:9; etc.), but it was also very specifically for me. I confess that sometimes that fact is harder for me to grasp. However, any being that can design DNA can care about seven billion people in a personal way, including me! A focus on his scars helps me keep that reality in mind.

I read in a biography of Winston Churchill that he identified easily with the great body of English people, but he couldn't get along with his gardener and other hired help. He was a genius in dealing with the English, but often a failure in dealing with an Englishman.

A preacher once told a friend that he loved the church but couldn't stand the people! Jesus wasn't like Winston Churchill or the preacher. He deals with great nations and masses of people, but he also deals very personally with me as an individual. The very hairs of my head are numbered (Luke 12:7).

"Accept Christ as your personal savior." Some have pointed out that this exact phrase isn't in the scriptures[20] and, of course, it isn't. Neither do those words make up a simple formula through which someone accepts Christ by a mental acknowledgement of him while ignoring other teachings he gives. However, it is possible to overreact to such abuses to equally an equally harmful extreme such as I found in a book that I like in some areas.

- "Having a personal relationship with Jesus is a hoax."[21]

- "No one was ever told to have a personal relationship with Jesus Christ, nor is the principle taught in the Bible."[22]

Though it is true that the exact phrase isn't found in the Bible
and that it is often abused, the fact remains that God wants a
very personal bond with us. (Just before publishing this book, I
received a much appreciated note on Facebook from the author
of the book I quoted, acknowledging that these comments might
be misunderstood. I appreciate very much his humility, but will
leave the quotes to illustrate a concept that many others have.)

Paul said, "… the life I now live in the flesh I live by faith in the
Son of God, who loved me and gave himself for me" (Gal. 2:20).
"He gave himself for me." There was something very personal about
Christ's death in the mind of Paul. Yes, it was for the masses,
but Paul saw it on a very personal level. It was for him! Christ's
wounds and scars were also for me on that personal level!

Jesus Christ worked primarily with individuals to establish a
personal bond with them. He was very personal with…

- Nathaniel when he saw him sitting under the tree (Jn.
1:48).

- The woman with the issue of blood (Mark 5:41).

- The widow who gave her two coins (Luke 21:1-4).

Jesus preached some of his greatest sermons to individuals—
Nicodemus (Jn. 3), the Samaritan Woman (Jn. 4), Martha at
Lazarus grave (Jn. 11). After His ascension Jesus saw Stephen
dying (Acts 7:56), the Ethiopian leaving Jerusalem (Acts
8:26), Cornelius among all the Gentiles (Acts 10), etc.

The religion of Jesus Christ is a very personal and intimate religion. His wounds and scars were for you and me! He looks upon us in a personal and intimate way and wants us to respond in that way to him. Yes, Christ wants to be our savior. He is not a distant force, but personal savior who wants close intimate bonds with us. His scars plainly show us that he has done all he can to establish that relationship. It is up to us now, to seek him.

Questions for reflection

1. Did those who beat and abused Jesus have any idea who he was? Do you see any comparison to people today who make fun of him and Christianity in general?

2. Have you sometimes contemplated what it would be like to have nails in your hands and heel bones, perhaps as you partake of the Lord's Supper? What are some descriptions you can think of to describe that kind of pain?

3. Have you ever seen a wounded and battered body, perhaps your own? It may be too graphic to describe. What does the fact that a pounded corpse would become a symbol of the love of the Creator of the universe mean?

4. What keeps us from seeing Christ's death as being for us on a personal level? What can we do to make it more personal for us?

5. What Bible example of Christ's dealing with one individual strikes you as especially moving?

Chapter 5

What Do the Scars of Jesus Say?

"I Have Been Raised"

"Put your finger here, and see my hands; and put out your hand, and place it in my side. Do not disbelieve, but believe" (Jn. 20:27).

Texts: Luke 24:36-43, John 20:19-29,

The little band of eleven Galileans who had followed Jesus must have been completely confused and bewildered as they huddled with their friends in the upper room immediately after the death of their teacher. They had dedicated almost three years of their lives to following him through the villages of Judea, Galilee, Perea and Samaria. They had seen startling miracles: Jesus walked on the water, raised a dead man who had been in his grave for four days and performed countless other signs that proved beyond a shadow of a doubt that He was from God. He talked to them often about God's kingdom that he would soon usher in.

Yes, there were many puzzling things about him. After talking about the imminent coming of the Kingdom he then talked about dying, two incompatible notions in the minds of his followers.

> And he began to teach them that the Son of Man must suffer many things and be rejected by the elders and the chief priests and the scribes and be killed, and after three days rise again. And he said this plainly. (Mk. 8:31,32a)

After hearing this seemingly defeatist language, Peter felt compelled to correct Jesus, the one he had just proclaimed to be the Christ, the son of the living God" (Matt. 16:16). "Peter took him aside and began to rebuke him" (Mk. 8:32b).

However, in spite of the puzzling and seemingly contradictory things Jesus said, his little band of followers still believed he was from God and perhaps even the Son of the Living God, though they often acted inconsistently with that truth, as we often do.

But then all their hopes came crashing down in a mind-spinning collapse. He was whisked away by Jewish leaders and subjected to the most degrading and humiliating death that could be imagined. And so, there they were—leaderless, hopeless and confused.

How depressing that Sunday gathering after Christ's death must have been! Perhaps there were a few embraces but it is more likely that they had already wrung out every tear and were simply sitting around in stunned silence.

Then some rumors began to filter into the room. The women who went to the tomb to prepare the body came and said that it was empty. What would that mean? They must have been even more puzzled when Mary Magdalene came in saying that she had actually seen Jesus and had talked to him (Jn. 20:18).

"No," they must have thought, "It can't be!" Then their male prejudices began to cloud their judgment, "No, these are just idle tales of women" (Luke 24:11).

But that wasn't the end of it. Simon Peter came in and said, "I saw him!" Shortly afterwards, two of their companions who had left in the late afternoon to go to Emmaus, came running in breathlessly saying that they had seen Jesus alive on the road.

Something is going on!

Yes, something was going on! At that very time a familiar figure appeared in front of them even though the doors were locked.

He spoke, "Peace be with you."

They might have been thinking, "No, it can't be. It must be his ghost!"

In spite of the testimony of the women and even that of Peter, Cleopas and his companion, the fact that their friend whom they seen as a cadaver three days earlier (as Jews counted time) was standing alive in front of them was more than their minds could handle.

Here his wounds showed their great significance.

> And he said to them, "Why are you troubled, and why do doubts arise in your hearts? See my hands and my feet, that it is I myself. Touch me, and see. For a spirit does not have flesh and bones as you see that I have." And when he had said this, he showed them his hands and his feet. (Luke 24:38-40)

Why did Jesus want them to focus on his hands and feet? That's where the wounds were. They must have just started to heal. To make sure that they understood that he wasn't a ghost, but really himself in bodily form, Jesus asked for a piece of fish and ate it in their presence.

What about poor Thomas? It was so difficult for him believe the unbelievable. For some reason he was not with his companions the Sunday after Christ's death, a point often made in traditional sermons on the importance of church attendance. When he saw his companions for the first time after they saw Jesus, they must have all rushed at him talking excitedly, "We have seen the Lord" (John 20:25A).

It all overwhelmed Thomas. He might have thought, "No, you must all be crazy! I saw him dead. Maybe there's a conspiracy going on around here."

He said, "Unless I see in his hands the mark of the nails, and place my finger into the mark of the nails, and place my hand into his side, I will never believe." (John 20:25B)

Eight days later the healing wounds again showed their significance. The apostles were again together. Jesus appeared in their midst and immediately zeroed in on Thomas. "Put your finger here, and see my hands; and put out your hand, and place it in my side. Do not disbelieve, but believe" (vs. 27).

Certainly Thomas must have been shaking with emotion and fear. The only words he could blurt out were, "My Lord and My God" (vs. 28).

The Resurrected Body of Jesus – The Heart of New Testament Preaching

Seeing the wounded body of Jesus resurrected from the dead lit a fire under the witnesses. Nothing—no political power, no torture, no abuse, no opposition could stop them from getting their message out—"We have seen the Lord" (Jn. 20:25).

The resurrected body that they saw became the heart of their teaching. There are at least 30 references to the resurrection in the book of Acts. It was the main theme in the sermons in Acts 2, 3, 9, 10, 13, 17, 20, 22, 23 and 26. Then there are well over 100 references to the resurrection in the rest of the New Testament.

The witnesses pressed the point again and again, even with hardened governors and kings. Paul challenged King Agrippa and his court, "Why is it thought incredible by any of you that God raises the dead?" (Acts 26:8) Paul had seen the risen Christ. His companions had seen him. He knew it had happened and you can almost sense his frustration at the fact that his royal listeners had already ruled out what he knew to be a fact before they listened to him.

The apostles could get very personal in their descriptions of their personal contact with Jesus. John said,

> That which was from the beginning, which we have heard, which we have seen with our eyes, which we looked upon and have touched with our hands, concerning the word of life… that which we have seen and heard we proclaim also to you…" (1 Jn. 1:1,3a)

Bible commentator Alfred Plummer, points out that the language in verse one about touching Jesus is practically the same as that used in Luke 24:39 and John 20:27. It indicates a direct reference to touching him after his resurrection.[23] It was an aggressive rebuttal to an ugly false doctrine (Docetism) that was already beginning to rear its head'—that Christ really didn't exist in the flesh, his wounds weren't real, his agony was only imaginary and whatever was raised, if anything, wasn't really a body.

"Oh yes! He did rise bodily from the grave!" John is saying. "We saw him, heard him and touched him."

Summarizing

There is much here we can't grasp. Where was Jesus from the time of his crucifixion to the time of his resurrection? Was he at times in paradise (Lk. 23:43) and then again at times present somewhere bodily on the earth as his wounds healed? Would he have been in both places at once? At what stage of healing were his wounds when he appeared on so many occasions to the apostles after his death and resurrection? How would his wounds have looked weeks later at his last appearance before his ascension? These must remain among the thousands of questions we'll have to ask in eternity. God chose not to reveal the answers to us.

However, the healing wounds of the risen Christ have left us with some startling truths to absorb.

* **His physical body was raised!** Jesus wasn't raised as a perfected heavenly body with no blemishes. His gashes still probably oozed blood. Since there were healing wounds, there were also white cells, red cells, plasma, corpuscles, etc. There were blood vessels, muscles, hairs, fingernails. It was not a ghost. It was his body and it was there.

So often it is easy to get into too much speculation about what all of this means, especially regarding our own resurrection and thus the theological theories start to fly. Paul dealt with this partially in 1 Corinthians 15, but he warned there about the dangers of too much conjecture (vss. 35, 36).

* **He is my Lord and my God.** That was Thomas' immediate conclusion and that's all that matters for us, theological speculation aside.

Sometimes we try to imagine how it would have been to literally see the risen Jesus. How would we have reacted? Though Jesus doesn't want to appear to us literally today, he appears to us through the testimony of the apostles and even doubting Thomas! As we read their accounts, we must judge their authenticity. Are these wild-eyed credulous accounts of those who had no idea what they saw? The more honestly we read and hear, the more we begin to have our own encounter with the resurrected Lord. If we keep honestly seeking, we will have our own "My Lord and My God" moment when we come to recognize fully who he is.

Questions for reflection

1. Why do you think that the apostles felt that Jesus was contradicting himself when promising on one hand that the Kingdom was coming and predicting his death on the other? Why do we find ourselves getting in over our heads when trying to explain what we feel to be somewhat contradictory biblical principles about the Kingdom? Might such apparent contradictions mean that it might be time to reevaluate our suppositions? Does it comfort you that Jesus was patient with the apostles as they worked through their misconceptions?

2. When have you been stunned and depressed as you spent time with a group of your friends? Can stunned depression come before triumph with us as it did with them? Who is the key to turning our stunned depression into triumph?

3. When have you been slow to believe?

4. Have you had a "My Lord and My God" moment like Thomas, an instance when it all came together in your mind about who Jesus is? Tell others about it if you like. Or, has truth dawned upon you more gradually? If such hasn't happened yet, what might be moving you towards acceptance of truth?

5. What are some characteristics of the testimony of the apostles about the resurrected Christ that indicate to you that it is trustworthy?

Chapter 6

What Do Jesus's Scars Tell Us?

"This Is How You Should Deal With Your Wounds."

"For to this you have been called, because Christ also suffered for you, leaving you an example, so that you might follow in his steps (1 Peter 2:21).

Text: 1 Peter 2:18-25

All adults are scarred by sin and the human experience. There are two types of scarred people: (1) those who are embittered and angry and (2) those who are loving and accepting. What better

way to make sure we are in the second category than to
imitate our Creator who came to earth?

Angry Christians

Todd Deatherage wrote about waiting in a carpool line
behind a Toyota 4-Runner whose "backside was plastered
with no less than 22 bumper stickers, three proclaiming the
driver's pro-life views, and three more in favor of gun rights."
Next to one prolife bumper sticker was one with a decal
image of an automatic assault rifle labeled as a "modern day
musket." Though Deatherage points out that he isn't a pacifist
or opposed to gun ownership he felt as if he were being
shouted at. [24]

Perhaps the 4-Runner belonged to one of my Facebook
friends. When I scroll down my wall, besides noticing the
usual family portraits and silly selfies, I see a number of Bible
verses and links to good articles but also a number of angry,
sarcastic comments usually directed at the president, the
liberals in Congress, illegal immigrants or refugees.

It is true that modern traditional Christian values along with
other Western traditions are under attack. To respond, some
advocate tactics such as joining "Christian" boycotts, anti-gay
ministries, Christian anti-communist groups and even anti-
Harry Potter clubs. You can always picket movies that have
anti-Christian themes. But was this Christ's way of dealing
with battle wounds and scars?

It's not that anger is always wrong. "Be angry and do not sin" (Eph. 4:26). Jesus threw the moneychangers out of the temple (John 2:13-22). God is angry at "all ungodliness and unrighteousness of men" (Rom. 1:18). However, "Christian" anger becomes a problem when it is misdirected and tactless. Christians often sin in their anger because they do not imitate their Master regarding the objects of their wrath nor the way they express it. They do not distinguish between righteous indignation and carnal retaliation.

The anger of Jesus was directed at Satan (John 8:44) and at religious people who were making a mockery of his Father's religion (Mark 3:5). It was not directed at those who personally hurt him. When he was attacked personally he worked to overcome that evil with good (Rom. 12:21). Unproductive Christian anger is often aimed at people of the world who oppose us on social issues, at politicians or perhaps at foreigners who we believe threaten our way of life. It is a "fight fire with fire" kind of anger that is counterproductive because it is not focused so much at Satan or his henchmen, but rather at those we feel have offended us personally or who provoke fear in us.

1 Peter 2:21-24

Peter gives a summary of the irrational anger directed against Christ by his enemies and then of his response to it. His motive was to encourage Christian slaves who were being abused.

He committed no sin, neither was deceit found in his mouth.

When he was reviled, he did not revile in return; when he suffered, he did not threaten, but continued entrusting himself to him who judges justly.

He himself bore our sins in his body on the tree, that we might die to sin and live to righteousness. By his wounds you have been healed.

The irrational nature of their anger #1 – "He committed no sin" (vs. 22a) – Peter refers here to Isaiah 53:9 and his emphasis is on the fact that Jesus suffered even though he had done nothing wrong.

Why do people of the world sometimes hate and ridicule the kindest Christians? There's often no logical reason. The author of the ancient letter of Mathetes to Diognetus pointed out that such was the case in the persecution of the earliest Christians in his beautiful chapter on "The Manners of the Christians."

They love all men, and are persecuted by all. They are unknown and condemned; they are put to death, and restored to life. They are poor, yet make many rich; they are in lack of all things, and yet abound in all; they are dishonored, and yet in their very dishonor are glorified. They are evil spoken of, and yet are justified; they are reviled, and bless; they are insulted,

and repay the insult with honor; they do good, yet are
punished as evil-doers. When punished, they rejoice as
if quickened into life; they are assailed by the Jews as
foreigners, and are persecuted by the Greeks; yet those
who hate them are unable to assign any reason for
their hatred.

The irrational nature of their anger #2 - Honesty (vs. 22b)
–"Neither was deceit found in his mouth." Liars hate truth
tellers. The leaders of Jesus' day hated Jesus not because of
his dishonesty or deception, but rather their frustration that
they couldn't find those flaws in him when they had so many
of them. His holiness and honesty made them look bad by
comparison and they hated him for that.

Three Keys to Dealing with Wounds

1. No retaliation (vs. 23a) – "When he was reviled, he did not
revile in return; when he suffered, he did not threaten."

As a teenager, I fantasized a little about being an expert in
some oriental martial art and being able to use it to whip all
kinds of villains. I suppose I was a little disappointed when
someone pointed out to me that most masters of the martial
arts rarely or never had to use their skills on bad guys. What
good is it to have great skill and power and then not use it?

Jesus Christ had the power to raise the dead and walk on the
water and yet when he was mocked, ridiculed and tortured
in the most unjust and inhumane way, he left all that power

as it were in his pocket. He told Peter, "Do you think that I cannot appeal to my Father, and he will at once send me more than twelve legions of angels?" (Matt. 26:53) Hymn writer Ray Overholt put it this way, in his hymn "Ten Thousand Angels" — "He could have called ten thousand angels to destroy the world and set him free… but he died alone for you and me."

Something deep within us wants to hurt others who have hurt us. Sometimes we fool ourselves by saying that all we want is justice. The desire for justice isn't wrong, but it can quickly convert itself into pursuit of carnal vengeance. That happens in particular when we begin to see ourselves as the primary enforcers rather than being content with God's enforcement, which he sometimes accomplishes through agents such as the government (Romans 13). Often when someone wrongs us, we feel the need to round up allies and proclaim our victimhood not to God and a few trusted spiritual friends, but to the whole world. That's simply not the way of Jesus.

2. Entrusting himself to the Father (vs. 23b)– He "continued entrusting himself to him who judges justly." This phrase recalls the words of Jesus in Luke 23:46, "Father, into your hands I commit my spirit!" Jesus refused to take matters into his hands. He simply committed himself to the father. John McArthur points out that the word "entrusting" literally means "'to hand over to someone to keep.' Literally, Jesus kept handing Himself and the circumstance of every unjust suffering over to God."[25]

An Illustration – Sexual Abuse

Our world's growing rejection of God increasingly fills it with sin and those who are victims of it. I have found myself dealing with an increasing number of sexual abuse victims during the past few ten years. Their justifiable anger is real and raw. It can quickly reach a boiling point and explode. Or, it can just sit there and simmer.

You've probably seen statistics like these regarding sexual abuse:

- 12% of all girls in grades 9-12 said that they were victims of sexual abuse.[26]

- One out of every six American women has been a victim of an attempted or completed rape during her lifetime.[27]

- According to *Cosmopolitan Magazine*, one in every three women between the ages of 18 and 34 has been sexually harassed at work.[28]

Modern psychiatry uses a number of tactics to try to treat the anger that comes from sexual abuse. Many seem counterproductive, causing the victims to constantly revisit the scene of the crime and reinforce their sense of victimhood.

Entrusting Ourselves to God

The way of Jesus is always best in the case of all emotional wounds, including those of sexual abuse. It is not to scream out or beat the wall to let frustrations out. Neither is it to seek vengeance or constantly revisit the hurt. In Jesus's case, there were two essential elements: (1) acknowledgement of what had happened to him and (2) entrusting himself to his father to handle the judgment.

That's exactly the medicine that God gave the Thessalonian Christians who suffered so much persecution from the very beginning of God's work among them (Acts 17). Paul told them in 2 Thessalonians 1:7-9.

> God considers it just to repay with affliction those who afflict you, and to grant relief to you who are afflicted as well as to us, when the Lord Jesus is revealed from heaven with his mighty angels in flaming fire, inflicting vengeance on those who do not know God and on those who do not obey the gospel of our Lord Jesus. They will suffer the punishment of eternal destruction, away from the presence of the Lord and from the glory of his might...

By the time the book of Revelation was written there were a number of martyrs who cried out for justice. "O Sovereign Lord, holy and true, how long before you will judge and avenge our blood on those who dwell on the earth?" (6:10). They were told simply to wait on God's judgment, in other words, to turn the matter over to him.

How practically can we entrust our wounds and slow healing scars to God? We do it through prayer and trust.

Prayer is the key as it was for Jesus, but not only for justice but also for healing for all involved. Even on the cross Jesus cried out for mercy for his tormentors (Luke 23:34). Stephen did the same thing (Acts 7:60). They asked for mercy, but left it in the Father's hand to determine how far and to whom to extend it. That's where trust came in. God didn't extend mercy to all of Christ's tormentors neither to those of Stephen. He still destroyed Jerusalem. While asking for mercy for their oppressors, both Jesus and Stephen trusted in God to determine how far to extend it.

Some people I've known have been able to kneel and with one fervent prayer ask God to take their hurt and work his justice or mercy according to his will. Through that one prayer they receive an almost instant spiritual healing and the grace they need. With most, however, entrusting their wounds to the father requires much more prayer over a period of time with gradual healing. But healing occurs. Though scars are left, they can gradually fade as we approach eternity.

3. Giving back to others – (vs. 24) "He himself bore our sins in his body on the tree, that we might die to sin and live to righteousness. By his wounds you have been healed."

Though Jesus was concerned about himself before his horrible death (Gethsemane, Jn. 12:27; 17:1-5, etc.) his primary concern continued to be for others. Even before being nailed to the wood, he lamented the coming punishment against Jerusalem (Lk. 19:41-44) and the suffering of the women of Jerusalem (Lk. 23:28-31). He spent much more time praying for his disciples in John 17 than for himself. He wanted to make sure that those who arrested him let his disciples go (Jn. 18:8). Then, while hanging in anguish, he was concerned about consoling the good thief (Lk. 23:43), his mother (Jn. 19:26,27) and even the well being of his tormentors (Lk. 23:34). A focus on others instead of an inward, "woe-is-me" approach to our pain and wounds is a key to our own eventual healing.

That's where our scars can be the most useful in the battle against evil—helping others who are dealing with the similar injuries by pointing them to the spiritual healing we have obtained through Jesus. Sexual abuse victims whose wounds have healed into scars will always be the most effective in helping other sex abuse victims. Alcoholics and drug abusers are in the best position to help other chemically dependent seekers turn their painful wounds into healing scars. No one wants to be placed in the ideal position to help others with painful wounds—that of veterans with scars from those same wounds. However, looking upon our painful injuries and disfiguring scars as powerful weapons we can use in the battles against Satan may make them more tolerable.

All disciples of Christ are sinners who have been healed from the wounds of sin. All of us are therefore capable of reaching out to others who are seeking spiritual and emotional healing. As we make written or mental lists of our suffering friends who need prayer in our minds or on paper, as we pour out our hearts to the Creator for them, as we contemplate their wounds to determine how best to help them and as we sacrifice to meet their needs, we find healing for ourselves.

It comes through imitation of the Master summarized in 2 Peter 1:23-25, (1) non-retaliation, (2) entrusting ourselves to God and (3) focusing on serving others. Thus we avoid the pitfalls of vengeance, uncontrolled anger and self-pity.

Questions for reflection

1. Why can angry Christians cause much harm if their anger isn't rightly directed and expressed? Can you give some examples without naming names?

2. What is the difference between "righteous indignation" and carnal anger?

3. What would it have been like to be a slave in the Roman Empire? Why do you think anger would have been a greater challenge for Christian slaves than for most of us?

4. What are some specific things you can do in prayer to help you to completely entrust your wounds to God? What keeps us from doing that and receiving the healing that comes from it?

5. What is a scar that you have that might make you especially qualified to help others who may be dealing with spiritual wounds? What can you do to use that "qualification" more effectively to help others?

Chapter 7

His Scars, Why Necessary?

"Therefore he had to be made like his brothers in every respect, so that he might become a merciful and faithful high priest in the service of God, to make propitiation for the sins of the people" (Hebrews 2:17).

Text: Hebrews 2:10-19

A young disciple named Beto Guerrero and I went to distribute gospel pamphlets with a brief gospel message to the throngs of people at the intersection of 145th Street and Broadway in New York City. I went to one corner and left Beto at the other. When I exhausted my supply of pamphlets, I crossed the street to find Beto listening to a man from the Dominican Republic, who was speaking so energetically, that Beto could hardly interject a word. I eased over to the two to try to understand what was being said, and realized that the man was denying that Jesus Christ was God.

"He was not God," he said emphatically. "There is only one God!"

"Oh," I thought. "This man is a Jehovah's Witness."

We didn't have much time left but thought I would quote him one verse that seems to give my Jehovah's Witness friends at least a little pause. So when the man finally paused ever so briefly for a breath of air, I interjected, "When Thomas saw the resurrected Lord in John 20:28, he said to him, 'My Lord and my God!' If Thomas could address Jesus as 'my Lord and my God,' (literally my 'the God') why shouldn't we?"

I expected a brief discussion of whether the text was directed to Jesus or just an offhanded exclamation, but what the man then said shocked me. "That man" (John) "was just a man like you and me. He was just giving his own opinion."

The man was no Jehovah's Witness! I believe that my Jehovah's Witness friends are mistaken, but they would never deny the inspiration of the apostle John.

I then asked, "If you reject the testimony of John and others who walked and talked with Jesus, whose testimony about Jesus will you accept?"

He replied, "I accept the testimony of the last great prophet, Mohammed."

The man was a Hispanic Muslim. What is the best way to have a mutually beneficial exchange with a Muslim in just a few minutes? I decided to emphasize the concepts about Christ's suffering found in Hebrews 2—in particular that God wanted to send his Son to earth, one with his same attributes, so that through suffering he could become our brother and perfect High Priest. We often talk of the resurrection of Christ in trying to help Muslims and others who don't believe in him, but his suffering is often linked with his resurrection and should also help persuade them (Matthew 20:18, 19; Mark 9:31; 10:33,34; Luke 24:25, 46; Acts 17:2,3; 26:22,23, etc.).

I emphasized that that God in coming to earth through his Son, Jesus, could therefore know what it was like to be human and share in the human experience.

That concept frustrated my new acquaintance. "God is our all knowing maker and designer!" he exclaimed. "How, by coming to earth, could he learn anything about the human experience since he already knows everything there is to know?"

I made a few more points about our relationship with God through Jesus Christ, but he wasn't impressed. Finally, we had to part ways amicably but mutually frustrated.

God's Perspective or Our Perspective?

I often beat myself up after discussions with those with other points of view, thinking I should have said this or should have said that. In thinking of how I could have communicated better with the Muslim I met, I realized that he was focusing on the fact that God didn't need to come to earth as Immanuel to learn anything about life under the sun from his own perspective. However, God did not send his son to come to earth to enrich his own perspective, but rather for ours. It wasn't enough for him to know the scarring human experience. He wanted us to know that he knows. That could only happen by personally injecting himself onto this planet. If Paul said that his scars were for our benefit (2 Cor. 4:15), how much more the incarnation (God coming to the earth in the flesh in the form of Jesus) was not for God's sake but for ours! I wish I had made this point clearer.

Sharing in Suffering, a Key to Helping Others

Not long after moving to New Jersey, I met an impressive and energetic young woman from El Salvador named Tonita. She and her husband, like millions of other Salvadoran immigrants in the 1980's and 1990's, fled war in her home country and were struggling to survive in an unknown culture with an unknown language. However, she was a determined and unstoppable woman. Her husband worked in a carwash. She contributed to the family income by going to upscale neighborhoods, knocking on doors and saying in broken English to any who would listen that she would clean their house for a very reasonable price.

I have often thought that it would have been tough for Tonita to obtain her first housecleaning jobs. It's not hard to imagine the surprise that prosperous residents of West Orange, New Jersey must have felt when seeing this diminutive woman often in native garb and accompanied by a baby at their door asking to enter into their homes. She must have been persuasive, however, because the word about her soon spread and in a very short period of time she had a rather large circuit of homes to visit and clean.

However, when Tonita's baby was one year old, he became sick with pneumonia and after a short stay in the hospital, died. Tonita was sure that the baby's death was caused in part by the negligence of the doctors because she and her husband, like most other immigrants, had no health insurance. She, of course, was heartbroken, and yet it wasn't her style to collapse in wails of anguish. Rather, with a resolute face she decisively made plans for her baby's burial as I accompanied her to a funeral parlor to help with the translation.

How my heart ached for Tonita! How could I help? I tried to tell her again and again that I was very sorry about the loss of her baby. I knew that Tonita appreciated my efforts but also knew that she was probably thinking, "You have no idea what it's like to lose a child." And she would have been right. I couldn't say that I knew what it was like to lose a baby, because thankfully that has not happened to me.

One who could have helped Tonita much more than I would have been someone, in particularly a mother, who had also experienced the loss of a child. However, I knew no such Hispanic mothers at that time who were in a position to help

Tonita. So, she stoically faced the greatest tragedy a mother can suffer, with only an occasional tear marring her stony face, thinking that no one around her really understood.

Tonita and her husband moved on after a year or so and I lost touch with her. I've often wondered about her, hoping that she has found in God the strength to come to grips with her loss. Perhaps she has been able to find another disciple who has suffered the same unspeakable hurt and receive solace from her, or perhaps she has found some level of healing by consoling others who have lost their babies.

No one can help others with various types of grief and scars like someone else who has experienced the same! That's why those who suffer from breast cancer, arthritis or other diseases seek out others who have suffered the same. Parents of autistic children or those with other special needs often meet together to share stories and learn how to deal with their unique challenges.

Christians can be thankful that theirs is not a God who stays comfortably ensconced in heaven, watching from a distance as his creatures struggle with their wounds. Rather, he is one who in the form of His Son has descended to share an incomprehensible measure of all the emotional and physical beatings that humans suffer. He shared in every way the anguish and emotional scarring that characterizes a world that is increasingly affected by the devastation of sin. He is a God who not only knows the battles that must be fought in this world, but also has wanted to make sure that we know that he knows. Therefore, we can confidently approach Him, seeking his consolation and hope. Through Jesus Christ, he has shown us that the wounds and scars are signs of love and also indicate that victory will soon be ours.

May God help me to express these truths more clearly to the next Muslim friend I meet and to all who see God as distant and severe so that they can come to know him as he truly is!

Questions for reflection

1. Have you ever had the opportunity to talk to a Muslim about your faith in Christ? What approach did you take to try to introduce him to the Way?

2. Why do you think some have such a difficult time imagining that the Creator of the universe has come to this earth to share the human experience? Could it be that they have a hard time grasping a love that could be so great? Do you have a hard time grasping it?

3. Are you a member of any support group for those suffering from a particular illness or trauma? Do you know anyone who is a member of such a group? Why can such be helpful?

4. How can fellow Christians be a kind of support group for us as we deal with the trauma of sin in our lives and on this earth? What sometimes keeps that from happening as it should?

5. Could we welcome Christ into such a "support group" of Christians, struggling to deal with sin? How can we do that? How can his coming to earth help us with that?

Part 2

Our Scars

Chapter 8

Our Good Scars!

Those That Come from Our Love

"Who is weak, and I am not weak? Who is made to fall, and I am not indignant?" (2 Corinthians 11:29)

Texts: 2 Timothy 4:9-18; Matthew 5:11,12

To love is to be scarred. The more you love, the more you'll be scarred. Love is the investment of ourselves in others – our time, our resources and emotions. The rejection of that love results in deep, penetrating emotional wounds. And yet, the scars that come from our love are good scars, divinely commanded scars, giver's scars. They identify us with our scarred Savior, wounded by the rejection of those he came to save. Anyone with few emotional scars from rejection is probably not much of a giver because scars often accompany giving.

Good Scars and Children

"Don't ever have kids," Elaine told me when I was a teenager. "They will break your heart!" Elaine (not her real name) had been a family friend for a number of years and her words had an impact on me. She had always seemed to be an optimistic and happy person. For her to speak so bitterly about having children, "the heritage of the Lord" (Ps. 127:3-5) speaks to the depth of grief that comes from their rebellion.

Godly parents often have unbelieving children. In that sense they are like God. "Listen, O heavens, and hear, O earth; For the Lord speaks, 'Sons I have reared and brought up, But they have revolted against Me'" (Isaiah 1:2).

We tend to blame ourselves when our children do not respond to God's love and it is always very easy to begin to dwell on some of our thousands of mistakes with them as the cause for their spiritual problems. And yet, if the perfect Father has rebellious children, so often will his flawed children.

Some rebellious children reach the depths of worldly depravity – drug addiction, abandonment of family, sexual predation, sexual perversion and the long list of Romans 1:28-32. Others simply stop seeking God by refusing to meet with his people but otherwise live orderly lives. Or, they drift into a watered down and convictionless approach to Christianity. Either way, their ungratefulness towards God leaves profound wounds and ugly scars on their earthly parents but even more on their Heavenly Father.

An older family friend named Mary told of raising her
teenage boys during the rebellious 1960's. She worked at an
upscale store in a shopping center when one of her sons came
to her section of the store to seek her help. He had grown his
hair out hippy style and wore the bell-bottom pants typical
of that era. Like others influenced by hippies, he was going
through a stage where he believed in the "natural approach"
to life— little bathing, deodorant or other efforts at personal
hygiene. She admitted that when she first saw him come
towards her at work she flinched, but then she told herself—
"He probably needs me now more than he ever has." So, she
dismissed herself from her high-class customers, gave him a
big hug in front of them, put her arms around him and asked
what she could do to help.

Mary has long since departed from this world, but her son,
after battles with alcoholism, is now humbly seeking God.
Though her son's rebellion scarred her, her loving response
to him in the midst of her pain (and his) must certainly be a
factor in his desire to seek God now.

I have a young Hispanic friend who began to talk to me
one day about all the rebellious, mixed up teenagers he
sees and the fact that the world is getting worse. "I don't
believe I'll ever want to have children," he told me. Such
pessimism is becoming increasingly common among
millennials.

Were Elaine and my young friend right? Does the potential
anguish that children can bring to parents mean that it is

better not to have them in the first place? Thankfully God doesn't take that approach! If the potential anguish of rebellious children meant never to have them, we wouldn't be here! Our world needs more children raised in the homes of disciples of the Lord in the middle of our perverse and crooked generation. That is true even though some of them may become casualties in the war between good and evil, between love and indifference.

The way of love is the way of God. It is to have children in spite of their potential rebellion and indifference, accepting the wounds and scars that come with the process. The scars that godly parents have because of their children's spiritual struggles are good scars, givers' scars, scars that identify them with the Creator.

Scars from Leadership

Marisol had been seeking Christ for several years before making a concerted effort to grow in Him by encouraging others, taking a lead in Bible studies and calling others to motivate them. Most responded well, but one misread her efforts to help as "trying to run the church." When the weaker Christian cited her efforts to "run the church" as a reason to stop attending congregational gatherings, the word got back to Marisol who was justifiably hurt,

"Why try?" she said. "When you put yourself out to help others they misread you and start to attack you."

"Welcome to the club," I told her, and then began to try to explain to her that the wound she was suffering, though painful, was a good wound that would turn into a good scar.

Those who push themselves to help others are the ones who will be most attacked. That was first true of Christ and then in turn with his followers (Jn. 15:18,19). It wasn't the weaker Christians who were beaten in the first century, but the apostles and the strongest witnesses. The Judaizing teachers didn't attack ineffective disciples. They set their guns primarily on Paul, the most effective evangelist in bringing Gentiles to Christ.

Sometimes leadership wounds and scars come not so much from evil people, but from those in whom we have invested much time and many tears. Paul's last letter, 2nd Timothy, mentions several people whom he had served at great costs, but who abandoned him when he needed them the most, just before his death.

- "You are aware that all who are in Asia turned away from me, among whom are Phygelus and Hermogenes" (1:15).

- "For Demas, in love with this present world, has deserted me and gone to Thessalonica. Crescens has gone to Galatia, Titus to Dalmatia" (4:10).

- "At my first defense no one came to stand by me, but all deserted me. May it not be charged against them!" (4:16).

Those who have never sought to lead never suffer the level
of rejection of those who put themselves out to sacrifice
for others. They never know this level of wounding and
scarring and wonder about the sanity of those they do, never
understanding that the scars that come from leading are good
scars, givers' scars.

Jesus gives us the key to dealing with leadership wounds
and scars in his prayer both in Gethsemane and in John 17,
pleading with the Father for His will to be done as he faced
the abandonment of his closest followers. Genuine, fervent
prayer is the best balm. Though his follower, Paul, knew the
pain of abandonment and indifference by those he had tried
to lead, he knew that as a follower of Christ, he was never
completely abandoned, "But the Lord stood by me and
strengthened me" (2 Tim. 4:17).

The Lord stands today by those who have been abandoned by
those they have taught. He heals them. As their wounds turn
into scars, they become easily identifiable with their spiritual
ancestors. What an honor!

Good Scars – Ridicule

There was once a time in Western Culture when the Bible
was generally respected and those who tried to follow it were
admired. No more! The flood of postmodern ideas pouring
into culture first through television and movies and now
through myriads of other channels has stamped 21st Western
culture with a decidedly anti-Christian imprint.

Postmodern propagandists have had a field day with language. They have been successful in instilling in most Westerners the idea that to promote virtue is to have a "phobia," to declare the need for high moral standards is to be judgmental and to point out the tragic results of grossly immoral behavior is to be a hater. Thus, what is good has become evil and what is evil has become good (Is. 5:20). And then, there are the clichés and trite sayings!

- "There is no such thing as absolute truth."

- "Words mean nothing."

- "I'm spiritual but not religious."

- A funny one I saw on Facebook - "I believe in a God who doesn't take religion seriously."

- One I understand, but it's taken too far, "I don't believe in organized religion."

The inherent inconsistencies in such platitudes mean nothing to most modern thinkers when their feelings carry more weight than reason, but they do clash with Christ's teachings.

- "I am the way the truth and the life, no one comes to the father but by me" (Jn. 14:6).

- "...He will speak words to you by which you will be saved... "(Acts 11:14).

This conflict between Christ and modern culture is played out every day in the lives of his followers as they deal with others in classrooms, the workplace and media. As they increasingly become a minority, they receive more insults— "fanatic," "Bible thumper," "prude," "intolerant," "self-righteous," etc.

Such opposition shouldn't surprise us since it reflects an eternal battle between good and evil.

• Today's world loves darkness (Eph. 5:3-5,11). Disciples proclaim the light.

• Today's world wants loaves and fishes. - Disciples offer the "bread of life" (Rom. 8:5).

• Today's world wants freedom from oppression. - Disciples offer freedom from sin (Rom. 6:1-18).

• Today's world wants a democratic religion. - Disciples recruit for a king with all authority (Mt. 28:18).

• Today's world wants traditions of men. - Disciples obey the commandments of God (Mt. 7:21).

Many media sources promote the anti-Christian agenda. An article on David Horowitz's "Discover the Networks" webpage states about Hollywood,

> Since at least the 1970s, the vast majority of Hollywood films dealing with Christians and their faith have portrayed

them in a harshly negative light. For the most part,
characters such as kindly priests and steadfast ministers
have disappeared from American cinema, supplanted by
what the author Donald Feder has called, "a rogue's gallery
of lusting priests, sadistic nuns, perverted pastors and con-
men TV evangelists – not to mention ordinary Christians
(Catholic or evangelical) who are depicted as superstitious
nitwits, malevolent hypocrites, or both."[29]

Many who loudly proclaim tolerance, learn to parrot the
anti-Christian propaganda that they hear and thus the hatred
against Christians grows. Modern society has come to reject
any kind of bigotry, except that which is directed against
Christians.

Being a victim of anti-Christian bigotry hurts! It leaves scars.
I'll give three personal examples I've heard of recently that
may not be earthshaking, but illustrate what is becoming
increasingly common in daily life.

• An old friend invited a young woman who just
became a Christian to dinner at a restaurant. When she told
him happily that she was now a Christian, he looked at her
with disdain and disbelief and walked out of the restaurant
without saying anything, leaving her to find her own ride
home.

• A friend of mine arrived early from out of town for a
Bible study that a local congregation had scheduled for him
to teach to a group of teens. He decided to stop with his

companion at a local McDonalds where they bought bottles of water, sat down and began to read the Bible quietly to prepare their minds for the study. Suddenly, the owner of the franchise stormed over angrily and asked them what they had bought. They showed him the bottles of water. That did not calm him. After making some sarcastic remarks about their reading the Bible in his restaurant he called some employees who reluctantly obeyed their boss and escorted my friend and his companion out of the restaurant.

- ·A mother whose daughter had determined to reject the skimpy PE outfit required by her high school, was dismayed when school officials and other students belittled her daughter's convictions as prudish. "It's unfair," cried out the mother, even as the daughter took the ridicule with more grace.

When considering the last example, I think of that fact that the indignation shown by some disciples as they deal with the wounds of anti-Christian ridicule is counter-productive and doesn't take into consideration the commands of their King!

> Blessed are you when others revile you and persecute you and utter all kinds of evil against you falsely on my account. Rejoice and be glad, for your reward is great in heaven, for so they persecuted the prophets who were before you. (Matt. 5:11,12)

When the ridiculers see their victims respond as Jesus did, not with anger or political slogans, but with love and kindness, a seed is planted that in the future may work change in them. It is still possible to overcome evil with good (Rom. 12:21).

Of course, the ridicule disciples suffer today, at least in the West, is often little compared to those Christians during the first few centuries after Christ. The power of a loving response to ridicule and even unspeakable torture was one of the keys in eating away the power of the cruel Roman Empire. It is still the only way to effectively deal with anti-Christian mockery of today and to turn painful ridicule wounds into healing scars. These are good scars, heroic scars and badges of honor that put us into the best company in history.

Questions for reflection

1. What are some "good" scars that you have, wounds that have come from trying to help others? If you have to stop and think a while, might that mean that there needs to be more sacrifices in the life you lead?

2. Have you ever known those who have become embittered by the rebellion of their children? Have you been tempted to become embittered yourself when you've had problems with your own? What characteristics of God can you point out to help them and help yourself?

3. Have you held yourself back when a leader was needed among disciples because you feared the criticism that would occur if you stepped forward? How can we best fight this tendency?

4. Can you give examples of anti-Christian bigotry that you or those close to you may have experienced?

5. When have you fallen into the "woe-is-me" mode when questioned or even ridiculed for your faith? What keeps us from rejoicing and being glad in such circumstances? How can we do better?

Chapter 9

Living Scars

Those That Come Simply from Living

"O Lord, God of my salvation; I cry out day and night before you. Let my prayer come before you; incline your ear to my cry! For my soul is full of troubles, and my life draws near to Sheol" (Ps. 88:1-3).

Texts: Luke 6:37, 38; 1 Cor. 15:42-44; Jeremiah 8:18 – 9:1

We live in a traumatized and scarred universe. The planets and their moons are pummeled with encounters from outside forces like asteroids and comets along with inner gashes caused by movements of tectonic plates. The same is true of its human inhabitants. We are forced to deal with injuries from without and within that leave us gouged and scarred. These are simply part of the historic battles between good and evil where love triumphs only through severe testing. When God chose to give man free will so that there would be love, He was also choosing to make a scar-filled universe.

The Creator knew that we must be wounded in battle before triumphing in his love. In the Bible He gives us the healing medication to deal with our wounds, through teaching, the examples of godly people but primarily through the model of His son.

We could make long lists of the sources of scars that comes simply from living on this planet, but will focus briefly on a few.

Scars from Imperfect Parents

You can rate human parents from 1-9 on a scale of 1-10. None, of course, reach 10 points. Very few would reach 8 or 9 points. Most of us hover in the "fair to middling'" range 4-7. A few simply don't care, are nonexistent or worse than any others, abuse their children sexually. Wherever parents fall short, they wound their children whom they love so much.

A brief list of common mistakes of well-meaning parents would include:

- Too much punishment

- Too little punishment

- Too much praise

- Too little praise

- Enabling laziness

- Too much pushiness

- Not enough time in prayer

- Not enough time in Bible study

- Too distracted with our own problems to give proper attention

- A failure to teach giving

- Bad examples when dealing with stress

Some of the best people in the Bible come across as being pretty bad parents, at least on occasions: Noah, Rebecca, Jacob, Eli, Samuel, David, Jehoshaphat, etc.

How to Deal with Scars from Our Parents' Mistakes

(1) **Mercy** – "Judge not, and you will not be judged; condemn not, and you will not be condemned; forgive, and you will be forgiven… For with the measure you use it will be measured back to you" (Luke 6:37, 38).

Our parents were often scarred themselves. If we want to receive mercy, we must work to cultivate a merciful attitude towards them in spite of all of their failings. Some parents may be so corrupt that even in our efforts to cultivate a merciful attitude, we should still maintain some distance from them. However, above all else, disciples of Jesus must follow him and avoid the vengeful spirit.

(2) Overcoming evil with good – "Do not be overcome by evil, but overcome evil with good" (Rom. 12:21).

A South American friend was abandoned by her father when she was five years old. She found herself harboring strong resentment for all the emotional damage caused by the separation. When she became a Christian she wondered how God would want her to deal with him. Then she heard that he had suffered some strokes and was practically helpless. She determined to go see him in Peru.

When she came into his room and saw the helpless little man lying on the bed, she determined to do everything in her power to follow Jesus and overcome his evil with good. She began serving him, patting his hand and calling him "Papacito" (daddy). At first he didn't know how to react, but very soon began to respond with the same tenderness he was receiving from her. He gradually recovered a little strength and lived a few years longer. The relationship she had with her father during his last years could be described by all the words that were lacking from her childhood: tenderness, affection, concern, acceptance and love. When he finally died, she knew that God had given her the healing she had always longed for by teaching her through the power of the example of his Son how to overcome evil with good.

(3) Focus on our heavenly Father. "And because you are sons, God has sent forth the Spirit of His Son into your hearts, crying out, "Abba, Father!" Therefore you are no longer a slave but a son, and if a son, then an heir of God through Christ" (Gal. 4:6,7).

The concept of God as our Father is unique to Christianity. Mary Kassians wrote,

> "Father" is the most significant name of the God of the Bible. It is the name that sets Christianity apart from all the other religions of the world. Other religions invite us to worship their gods, allahs, creators, or metaphysical forces, but Christianity invites us to believe in a Son and to enter into an intimate family relationship with a loving Father. [30]

Though our earthly parents will have many flaws, our heavenly Father has none. Though the mistakes of our earthly parents may leave scars, a focus on our perfect heavenly Father and a trust in his healing and nurturing power can fade those scars quickly.

(4) **Optimism** - That relationship with our heavenly Father takes away the depressing focus on our past victimhood and places it on the glorious future we will have with him. We don't have to be oppressed by past memories, but rather liberated by the anticipation of future glory.

Scars from Imperfections in Our Bodies

The statistics and anecdotal evidence confirm that fact that Americans are not happy with their bodies.

- Currently, 80 percent of women in the U.S. are dissatisfied with their appearance. And more than 10 million are suffering from eating disorders.[31]

- According to the National Eating Disorders Association, 42 percent of first- to third-grade girls want to lose weight, and 81 percent of 10-year-olds are afraid of being fat.

- I remember hearing a somewhat overweight preacher say from the pulpit, "I absolutely despise my body."

Much of the dissatisfaction with our bodies comes from the images we see in the media. Perfectly proportioned models flit happily across various types of screens selling not only all kinds of products but also the lie that happiness depends on having physical bodies like theirs.

Dr. Carolyn Coker Ross writes,

> Herein lies the real damage. The more an individual is exposed to the media, the more he or she believes it is reflective of the real world. What most people still don't realize is that the majority of the pictures they see in magazines are altered in some way and that looking like their role models is physically impossible. It is a setup for self-hatred.[32]

Young people think, "I'm never going to have a boyfriend," or, "I'm never going to have a girlfriend." It seems to them that someone else is always receiving the attention they crave so much from the opposite sex and it's all because they're too fat, skinny, short, tall, big nosed, big eared or whatever. The obsession with body flaws also affects those who are older as they stare into the mirror noticing their increasingly wrinkled skin, age spots, gray hairs, less hair on the head and more in the nose and ears.

What are some principles that God gives us to help us deal with the emotional wounds and scars that come from our imperfect bodies?

1. It was never God's intention that our bodies be perfect. Job called our bodies "houses of clay" (4:19) and Paul called them "jars of clay" (2 Cor. 4:17). They are perishable (1 Cor. 15:53). If our bodies were perfect, we would have no reason to seek anything better. They were designed to give us a temporary dwelling place where we can show our love for God so that we can receive something much better.

Even those famous celebrities who seem to have flawless bodies have their imperfections. The images we see of them are enhanced with Photoshop manipulation, cosmetics and plastic surgery. As pretty as they seem to be, sooner or later they will have to accept the reality that accompanies the aging process that leads to death.

2. Although we should take care of our bodies (1 Cor. 6:19), we should be much more concerned with perfecting our souls. The care we give our bodies should not develop into the obsession of the narcissist. They are "tents" (2 Cor. 5:1). Therefore, "while bodily training is of some value, godliness is of value in every way, as it holds promise for the present life and also for the life to come" (1 Tim. 4:8).

Some people who have disfigured bodies are beautiful inside. You know some! Although all of us can't be pretty physically, every one of us can be beautiful on the inside as we develop our character, love, service and humility.

3. We're going to receive a perfect body.

- "For we know that if the tent that is our earthly home is destroyed, we have a building from God, a house not made with hands, eternal in the heavens" (2 Cor. 5:1).

- "What is sown is perishable; what is raised is imperishable. It is sown in dishonor; it is raised in glory. It is sown in weakness; it is raised in power. It is sown a natural body; it is raised a spiritual body. If there is a natural body, there is also a spiritual body" (1 Cor. 15:42-44).

Though we don't know exactly what that body will be like (1 Jn. 3:2), we know that it will be perfect, without defect and eternal. Instead of worrying so much about our temporary bodies, we need to contemplate the perfect and eternal ones we will receive.

4. Focus on blessings. A good medicine for any kind of depression is to go back and think of our great blessings: life, the senses, the beauty of nature and most of all, the fellowship we can have with God and his people. The advice of the old hymn, "Count your Blessings," is still good!

> Count your blessings, name them one by one;
> Count your blessings, see what God hath done;
> Count your blessings, name them one by one,
> And it will surprise you what the Lord hath done.

When we become discouraged with our imperfect bodies, that's a good time to go to the park, the woods or some place where we can surround ourselves with the beauty of God's creation. It's a good time to go to a nursing home and visit with the elderly or to a hospital to visit a sick brother. It's a good time to gather with Christian friends to sing and pray. Those are ways God can give us perspective. After five seconds in God's presence in eternity, we will have forgotten all about being too fat, too skinny, too tall or too short. Those scars will all be gone!

Scars from Broken Marriages

A friend tried to describe his pain from his divorce in verse, including the following lines.

> I feel pain in the depths of places that did not exist before.
> I have cuts where once I never did.
> I don't know how these cuts can heal.

Dr. Andra Brosh described her emotional state after her divorce.

> When my marriage ended a few years ago, I felt like I had been run over by a truck. I wandered through the world silently wounded with an invisible arrow through my heart. I was in a daze, life felt surreal, and my mind, body and spirit were broken.[33]

Those of us who have not suffered the trauma of a broken marriage can only try to imagine the overwhelming feelings of rejection, loneliness and perhaps even guilt suffered by an increasing numbers of believers who have gone through that misery. Though we can't understand the depth of the hurt, we can point our brethren and friends to the one who does – Jesus Christ. Christ is rejected on a daily basis by millions who see his coming to earth and his shed blood as either fantasy or of little importance. And yet, he keeps on loving and reigning.

God considered his relationship with ancient Israel as that of a marriage and described in the prophets the unspeakable pain caused by the rupture of that marriage. One of the more graphic descriptions of God's grief is in through his words given to Jeremiah in chapter 8.

• "My joy is gone; grief is upon me; my heart is sick within me." (8:18).

• "For the wound of the daughter of my people is my

heart wounded; I mourn, and dismay has taken hold on me"
(8:21).

- "Oh that my head were waters, and my eyes a fountain
of tears, that I might weep day and night for the slain of the
daughter of my people" (9:1).

These words sound like those of my friends whose marriages
have become irreparably broken. God knows rejection. He
knew he would have to learn it when creating beings with free
will. However, he still chose to make us and to love us. The
same is true of those who chose to love in marriage and then
suffer rejection in it. Perhaps in this sense they can identify
more closely with the Creator than those of us who have been
blessed never to suffer that level of rejection.

That is perhaps a key for coping with all of our wounds and
scars that come simply from living—a focus on the fact that
they identify us with our rejected and scarred Creator and
help us prepare to live eternally with him.

Questions for reflection

1. What were some of your parents' strengths? What were
some of their weaknesses? (Use discretion in discussing the
latter in a group setting.)

2. What might be a barrier to having a merciful attitude
towards them regarding their weaknesses?

3. Do you have some friends who have learned to be optimistic and full of hope in spite of deep wounds from their parents? What have been some of the keys to overcoming their rough upbringing?

4. What do you most dislike about your body? What biblical principle most helps you to keep that flaw in perspective?

5. Why are broken marriages so traumatic? How can God's response to his "broken marriages" with Israel and with others who fall away help us?

Chapter 10

Scars from Our Sin

"Purge me with hyssop, and I shall be clean; wash me, and I shall be whiter than snow" (Ps. 51:7).

Texts: Psalm 51; Titus 3:4,5

Our most painful wounds, the deepest gashes and the scars that most disfigure our appearance come from our own sin: our careless words, presumptuous acts, lack of self-control and especially our empty pride. And yet, many of the greatest heroes of the Bible were some who were horribly mutilated by their sin. God gives emphasis to their stories to show us that no depravity is too great for His grace, no wickedness too deep for His mercy.

• **Rahab the harlot** – Because she believed in the God of Israel, He chose her to became an ancestor of Jesus Christ. God's "Hall of Fame" in Hebrews 11 gives her prominent mention (vs. 31).

• **David**, the "man after God's own heart," was also an adulterer and murderer (2 Sam. 11). His presumptuous census, evidently an outgrowth of his pride, resulted in the death of thousands of Israelites (2 Sam. 24). That God could forgive him gives us pause at first and then wonderment at the power of His mercy and grace.

• **Peter's** continual "foot-in-the-mouth" disease makes him come across as a kind of shallow blabbermouth during the lifetime of Jesus. However, his denial of Christ and the resulting wound from that experience was a part of the package that changed him dramatically into one of the most valiant and straightforward defenders of the faith.

• Perhaps the apostle **Paul** was the worst. Only the cruelest of the cruel could go into homes to drag fathers and mothers away from their tearful children to prison (Acts 8:3). To actively participate in the gory spectacle of the stoning of Stephen would have required a mindset that is difficult for sheltered twenty-first century minds to grasp (Acts 7:54-60).

Though after his conversion Paul worked to forget those revolting crimes (Phil. 3:13), he was constantly aware of the depths from which Christ had raised him. He told Timothy in his first letter, "The saying is trustworthy and deserving of full acceptance, that Christ Jesus came into the world to save sinners, of whom I am the foremost" (1 Tim. 1:15).

Paul also knew why God chose to show him mercy. "But I received mercy for this reason, that in me, as the foremost,

Jesus Christ might display his perfect patience as an example to those who were to believe in him for eternal life" (1 Tim. 1:16). If God could show mercy to Paul, he could show anybody mercy! His sin scars became just as prominent in his testimony as his physical scars. They still speak to us today.

Untransformed Rahab, David, Peter and Paul have their modern day equivalents. Maybe we are all Rahab, David, Peter and Paul, but the good news is that we can be transformed just as they were.

Scars from Sexual Sin

God hates sexual sin. It profanes a sacred trust that God reserves for husband and wife, a symbol of his relationship with his people and a preview of heaven, and turns it into a cheap momentary thrill. It leaves lasting wounds and scars and is a common symbol in the Old Testament prophets of Israel's treachery and unfaithfulness towards God.

The wounds of sexual sin are sometimes slow to heal. One godly young man confided in me that though he has happily married to a sweet and beautiful young bride, images of pornography he sought as a child and teenager still haunt him and even now he still occasionally finds himself going back to seek them. In that sense his wounds haven't healed over yet. The scarring process isn't complete. Another middle-aged disciple disclosed that memories of old affairs still disturb him even though God's word has guided him to a wonderful woman.

As painful and durable as the wounds of sexual sin can be, God provides healing. A godly woman confided on *Facebook*:

> When I was a teen, I was caught up in the "When God Writes Your Love Story," and "I Kissed Dating Goodbye" craze that swept through evangelical teenage female lives and graced many pink bedroom shelves. I believed I would *never* fall prey to sexual sin - I would never even kiss a man before I married him. I was too strong. "True love waits," I thought, and I was sure I would wait. After all, I had The Truth. I knew what the Bible said. I was good at obedience. And yet, all of my strength, all of my reading, all of my preparation, all of the teaching I had received wasn't enough. Almost ten years ago, I met the man who would be my undoing. He flirted, cajoled, and flattered me until I gave in. When we broke up seven months later, I was used and broken, a virgin only in a technical sense.

Though God gave her "a period of blissful healing... the guilt came back over and over." Then she read a paragraph in a blog publication by Serena DeGarmo.

> It's true you will never restore your first purity. But I fear we may be giving this sin too much power. It is a sin. It is not an unforgivable sin. When we accept it, truth is that the blood of the lamb covers it, restores it, heals it and redeems it. That means we get a second chance. We get a new life. We get spiritual purification.[34]

Trusting in God's spiritual cleansing is the key to allowing all spiritual wounds to heal into spiritual scars. That, of course, is much easier said than done. Perhaps our problem is that we want to equate spiritual cleansing with removing temporal consequences. That, of course, is not always possible.

Temporary Consequences Versus Eternal Life

Cheri is a generous friend from South America who was so busy in her work that she didn't pay much attention to a small lump under one of her ears. However, it grew quickly and its size began to alarm her, so she made an appointment with a doctor. The doctor realized it was a fast-growing tumor that was already beginning to affect her brain and by the time he was able to arrange for surgery it had become an ugly mass affecting the whole side of her face. Cheri began to make plans to die.

The surgery was more complicated than expected and the surgeon had to detach large sections of muscle and skin to remove the tumor. However, he was able to get rid of it all and it was benign! Cheri began a long and slow rehabilitation that continues until now. The side of her face has been permanently deformed, but she is alive! She has been saved. Death is not imminent, though she must deal with some disfigurement and the loss of some neurological functions for the rest of her life. However, she's happy and relieved because she has been given a new lease on life.

Sin threatens our very spiritual existence. It can quickly take over our whole being. Nevertheless, when we go to the great physician, He removes our sin through his unfathomable grace and mercy.

However, some sins, just as Cheri's tumor, leave us permanently scarred and disfigured. Our reputation among men may be damaged. We may have harmed our marriages or other social relationships to the point that they cannot be recovered. We may have to choose to remain unmarried if we have gone through an unbiblical divorce and cannot be reconciled to our spouse (1 Cor. 7:11).

As the young woman referenced earlier who wrote about her sexual sin, sometimes we long to return to the completely unscarred state, but such isn't possible in this life. She can never be a virgin, as she put it, "in the technical sense," but she has been made alive! Her past sin no longer threatens her but has been completely put away. Like my friend Cheri, she can rejoice in her renewed life, though some scars remain from her sin. And, in the spiritual sense, God has made her a virgin again, completely cleansed and pure as snow.

We may be tempted to yearn for what God hasn't promised—removal of scars, all earthly consequences of our sin. If we drive while intoxicated, crash our car and lose a limb, we will be forgiven if we turn to God in repentance. Though we may want God to restore our lost limb, he doesn't promise that. He does promise to give us life, to heal us spiritually and to even use the thorn from our sin to bless others. Trusting in that fact helps us to deal with painful earthly consequences that remain.

Just as my friend Cheri rejoices in her unexpected extension of life, even though she must deal with some permanent leftovers of her battle with a tumor, so we can rejoice in our eternal life in Christ to the point that our temporary scars that remain from our battles with sin, don't really matter that much.

The Analogy of Washing

The scriptures often speak of the removal of our sins by the grace of God as washing.

- "Purge me with hyssop, and I shall be clean; wash me, and I shall be whiter than snow" (Ps. 51:7).

- "Wash yourselves; make yourselves clean; remove the evil of your deeds from before my eyes" (Isaiah 1:16).

- "Husbands, love your wives, as Christ loved the church and gave himself up for her, that he might sanctify her, having cleansed her by the washing of water with the word" (Eph. 5:25, 26).

- "But when the goodness and loving kindness of God our Savior appeared, he saved us, not because of works done by us in righteousness, but according to his own mercy, by the washing of regeneration and renewal of the Holy Spirit" (Titus 3:4,5).

For this reason baptism is given such importance in the scriptures. Ananias told Saul of Tarsus, "And now why do you wait? Rise and be baptized and wash away your sins, calling on his name" (Acts 22:16). Saul needed that cleansing of baptism, not as a mere symbol of something that had already occurred in his life, but as Peter described it - "an appeal to God for a good conscience, through the resurrection of Jesus Christ" (1 Pet. 3:21).

The story of the Philippian Jailor in Acts 16 illustrates this analogy. After participating either directly or indirectly in the mistreatment of the apostle Paul and Silas and then hearing the words of life about Jesus Christ, "he took them the same hour of the night and washed their wounds; and he was baptized at once, he and all his family" (Acts 16:33). The washing of their physical wounds, a washing of repentance, preceded his own washing in baptism, his spiritual appeal to God for a good conscience.

We need that washing today, both the washing of baptism to put us into Christ (Galatians 3:26, 27) and then the continuing cleansing of the blood of Christ as we confess our sins (1 Jn. 1:7). As we picture the blood of Christ flowing over us removing every bit of spiritual dirt, giving us renewed life; we understand that any temporary consequences that remain from our sin are bearable, and in fact trivial, compared to the glory of eternal life that God has planned for us. Thus wounds quickly heal into scars, scars that gradually fade as the years pass and as eternity draws near.

Scars from Illness and Death

We try to sanitize death. We understate it, hide it and cover it with music and flowers. Our need to soften the word "death" is reflected in the hundreds of euphemisms for it. An article on Lebanon Valley College's web page lists over 200.[35] Chris Raymond lists 101.[36] Here are a few more common ones:

- Pass away

- In repose

- Laid to rest

- Kicked the bucket

- No longer with us

- Biting the dust

- Gone to that great _____ in the sky

A few of these are humorous. Humor is often a way of managing pain. Perhaps some are necessary as coping mechanisms, but the Bible doesn't treat death or illness leading to death as something smooth and tolerable but rather as a cruel enemy that God is battling and defeating (1 Cor. 15:54-56).

I am thankful for modern medicine. It eased the pain for my mother-in-law who died this year of a brain tumor, helped my father cope with his compound fracture and helps my wife with her lupus flares. When I think of the easing of their pain, I think often of the fact that such relief wasn't available for most people in the history of the world. I thought when observing my father, "What about those who suffered compound fractures before modern medicine?" Many must have died slow and agonizing deaths. It is unsettling to read of the surgery and amputations performed on injured soldiers in the Civil War without any anesthesia.

Perhaps Christians are tempted to understate the awfulness of illness and death because they are used by unbelievers to attack the concept of a loving God—"How could a just and loving God permit all of this?" Then, we think of those who have turned against the concept of God when observing suffering and death, for example, Charles Templeton whose loss of faith after seeing a picture of a starving child was analyzed with such poignancy in Lee Strobel's classic, *The Case for Faith.*

Television mogul Ted Turner talked about his loss of faith.

> I lost my religious belief when my sister got lupus... She was 12 and she died at 17. I was 15 when she got it. She was ill. It ruined her mind. She became insane. She used to go around the apartment and run into the padded walls and say, "God, I'm in such pain. Please let me die."[37]

However, if Christians try to play down pain and death, we aren't like God. In coming to this earth through his son Immanuel, he acknowledged them and even embraced them, but also showed the way to deal with them. That's our only hope for dealing with the wounds of pain and death—acknowledging their existence while focusing on the only workable way the world has ever known of dealing with them—placing ourselves in the hands of our loving Creator who promises eternal relief.

Instead of trying to analyze all the unknowable reasons behind suffering and death, we do better to focus on the remedy. When unbelievers focus on the package of pain and death as a reason to cast off faith, we need to challenge them about the best way to confront it: (a) with the uncertainty and futility of unbelief that they are promoting? Or, the hope that comes from the Creator? Belief in God provides hope even for those who suffer in the deepest poverty and most agonizing pain. Rather than wallow in self-pity or shake our fist at God for what we don't understand, better to seek him and the hope he offers.

The fact that there is hope in pain only in God doesn't prove that he exists. However, something within us rebels against the thought that the marvel of our astounding bodies made up of cells of incomprehensibly complex DNA is the result of a meteorite strike and countless genetic accidents. We instinctively protest the concept expressed by atheist Bertrand Russell that man's "origin, his growth, his hopes and fears, his loves and his beliefs are but the outcome of accidental

collocations of atoms…"[38] Isn't there more to our existence?
What is the source of that instinct that makes us intuitively
know that there is more to our existence than a meaningless
second in eternity? God wants us to seek him and he is worth
seeking! He promises that those who honestly seek him will
find him (Matt. 7:7). "He is actually not far from each one of
us" (Acts 17:27).

Christians I have known generally take one of two courses
when confronting illness, suffering and death. They either
abandon God and therefore all hope, or they turn closer
to the one who knows that package personally better than
anyone else. In doing so they find healing and purpose. The
latter is the only real solution that allows open wounds to
gradually turn to scars that then begin to fade.

Questions for reflection

1. Have you ever wondered why God considered David to be
so faithful when he committed so many horrendous sins in his
life? Do you know any modern day "Davids," those who have
committed many errors and yet return to the Lord with complete
dedication? When in your life have you been like David?

2. Who are some modern-day "Sauls of Tarsus," bitter enemies
to Christianity? Could any possibly become Christians? Do you
know of any like him? Why is it so important not to be personal
and insulting when answering modern day Sauls who attack the
Bible and Christians? Have you been tempted to speak harshly
to atheists? To Muslims? To others who are in error?

3. Who do you identify with most: Rahab, David, Peter or Saul of Tarsus/Paul?

4. Do you have sin scars that you would like to be rid of? How can you put these sin scars into perspective when considering the blessings in Christ?

5. Are there some wounds of others that you need to "wash" – wounds you have inflicted either intentionally or unintentionally on others? How can you do that?

6. Why is a focus on the cause of suffering and death less helpful than a focus on the remedies for them?

Chapter 11

"My Grace Is Sufficient for You"

"But he said to me, "My grace is sufficient for you…" (2 Corinthians 12:9)

Text: 2 Cor. 12:1-10

I was walking down the halls of a hospital in Passaic, New Jersey when my attention was drawn to a crowded room of 15-20 people from rural Mexico. They surrounded the bed of an elderly man who was thrashing around in pain.

"What's going on?" I asked.

"He's dying of cancer," said a family member.

"Why don't they give him something to relieve his pain?" I asked.

That question was met with unknowing shrugs.

I think I know what was going on. The poor man probably had no health insurance, and that meant little medical attention.

I went into the hall and searched for a doctor and begged him to give the man something for his pain. He assured me that he would. I hope it was more than Tylenol. To this day, when I think of pain, I think of the little man writhing in pain surrounded by stoic family members.

When the pain hits closer to home, it has an even bigger impact! I remember my wife thrashing around in agony during a lupus flare. One of her doctors said that he had never seen an inflammation rate in the blood as high as hers. I remember my daughter's quiet tears after falling on the ice as I saw her broken upper arm hanging at an odd angle.

We all have our images of pain that we've seen in others and even experienced ourselves – intense, unbearable, agonizing! When seeing it or experiencing it we seek only one thing—relief! But, it isn't always forthcoming.

Paul's Thorn in the Flesh

God gave Paul many special privileges. He mentioned a special vision that God gave him of heaven in 2 Corinthians 12:1-6. But immediately after the story of the vision comes the story of the thorn.

> So to keep me from becoming conceited because of the surpassing greatness of the revelations, a thorn was given

me in the flesh, a messenger of Satan to harass me, to keep
me from becoming conceited. (vs. 7)

Interpretations abound regarding Paul's thorn in the flesh.
The book of Galatians hints at eye problems (4:15; 6:11) but
whether this was what Paul had in mind when referring to
his thorn is unknown. Various commentaries mention speech
impediments, headaches and other assorted maladies. Sir
William Ramsey suggests malaria.[39] Still others propose that
Paul's thorn refers to rejection by the Jews or problems with
difficult individuals. The fact is that the Holy Spirit didn't
want Paul to specify his thorn, perhaps so that we could more
easily apply the principles in the passage to our own varied
list of thorns. 2 Corinthians chapter 12 shows that the thorn
was painful, had bothered Paul for a long time and he was
incapable of getting rid of it.

Paul did all that he knew to do to deal with it. Just as Jesus
prayed three times in Gethsemane for his cup to be removed,
Paul said, "Three times I pleaded with the Lord about this,
that it should leave me" (vs. 8). Surely that didn't mean that
Paul simply mentioned it briefly in prayer three times, but
probably refers to three long sessions of prayer, perhaps
accompanied by fasting.

God loved Paul! What was he going to do about this thorn
and Paul's fervent prayer about it?

"But he said to me, 'My grace is sufficient for you...'" (vs. 9)

God didn't remove the thorn. He simply pointed Paul to the only thing that really mattered—His grace!

God's Grace, Always Big!

You never read in the Bible about "a little of God's grace," or "some grace." It's always big and abounding! Notice the following with italics added for emphasis:

- **Ephesians 1:7, 8** – "We have the redemption through his blood, the forgiveness of our trespasses, according to… the *riches* of his grace, which he *lavished* upon us."

- **1 Timothy 1:14** – "…the grace of God *overflowed* for me…"

- **2 Corinthians 9:8** – "And God is able to make all grace *abound* to you…"

- **2 Corinthians 9:14** – because of the *surpassing* grace of God upon you…"

We usually think of grace in terms of salvation from sin and that's correct - "For by grace you have been saved through faith, and that not of your own doing, it is the gift of God." (Eph. 2:8,9). However, it is possible to save someone without approving of them. Occasionally an intoxicated person falls onto the subway tracks in New York City and a Good Samaritan will jump down onto the tracts and save him. He saves the individual though not approving of his behavior.

God, however, not only saves us, but also through the blood of Christ approves of us and gives us a place of honor in His kingdom. "In the exercise of His will He brought us forth by the word of truth, so that we would be a kind of first fruits among His creatures" (James 1:18).

After all the stumbling and bumbling of his disciples during his lifetime, Jesus turned around and thanked the Father for them! John 17:6 has been an astonishing passage to me ever since I took special notice of it in my youth. There, Jesus poured out his feelings to His father about those unimpressive men the father had given him. "I have manifested your name to the people whom you gave me out of the world. Yours they were, and you gave them to me, and they have kept your word."

"They have kept your word."

Jesus goes on to give his Father lavish thanks for men we would describe as weak as water during his ministry.

How could Jesus be so thankful for those who had given him so much grief and whom he had scolded on so many occasions, "Oh you of little faith"? How could he say that they had obeyed the Father's word? Sometimes Bible students get into a deep theological and philosophical mode when answering this type of question, but the best approach is to simply say that the only explanation is grace, not little grace but marvelous grace, abounding grace, infinite grace! Jesus Christ didn't just save His disciples. He glorified them and approved of them.

We feel a strong urge to receive approval from those we admire.
I tried to play basketball for my tiny high school when I was
a teenager, but spent most of the time on the bench. I would
do almost anything to hear my coach say, "Hey Gardner, great
job! Keep it up!" Since he was a good motivator, though a bit
crazy at times, he did say it occasionally.

Preachers appreciate it when others try to give them
encouragement after a sermon. The comments range from the
dutiful, "appreciated the lesson" to the obviously exaggerated,
"that's the best sermon I've ever heard in my whole life." I
especially value reinforcement after a sermon when it is
measured, sincere and comes from mature Christians and
those who know what it's like to prepare a Bible lesson.
However, the most treasured compliments come from those
who are closest to us - "Son, that was a good effort."

However, nothing can compare to the thought that the Savior
of the world can look at me in spite of my failings and say,
"Father, I am glorified in Gardner." He said that of his apostles
(John 17:10) and He can say that of me! That's grace! That's
marvelous grace and abounding grace!

I have not had to suffer as much as my wife, my father
or others who must deal daily with agonizing thorns and
disfiguring scars. If one day, I must deal with such, I pray for
the strength to see God's grace as all sufficient. After my life
ends, after five seconds in God's immediate presence, all the
wounds and scars of this life will be as nothing. Then I will
see more clearly than ever, that His grace is sufficient for me.

When We Don't See That His Grace Is Sufficient

Since our world is so focused on material things, popular preaching has often become filled with a this-worldly focus on money and physical health rather than the grace of God. With Google you can find any number of quotes from popular preachers that emphasize health and welfare rather than God's grace.

• "Some people come to me and say, 'I came here to seek peace and not money.' I tell them, 'You need money or you're not going to have peace.' Some people say that it all has to do with peace, joy and love. No, it all has to do with money."

But Jesus says, "My grace is sufficient for you."

• "If you are struggling economically, you don't have victory."

But Jesus says, "My grace is sufficient for you."

• "If you take that into your spirit you will reach millionaire status in three years."

But Jesus says, "My grace is sufficient for you."

The fact is that God never promises material prosperity or physical health. Verses that are sometimes quoted to say that He does are taken out of context and ignore the simple fact that early disciples were generally poor. "For consider your

calling, brothers: not many of you were wise according to
worldly standards, not many were powerful, not many were of
noble birth." (1 Cor. 1:26)

Christianity was without doubt "a movement of the
impoverished classes."[40] Paul wrote in 2 Corinthians 8:1,2
about the "extreme poverty" of the Macedonian churches that
was well known.

> We want you to know, brothers, about the grace of God
> that has been given among the churches of Macedonia,
> for in a severe test of affliction, their abundance of joy
> and their extreme poverty have overflowed in a wealth of
> generosity on their part. (2 Corinthians 8:1,2)

However, he goes on to reason that they had "abundance"
in comparison with the "lack" of the Jerusalem Christians
(8:14).[41]

Jesus said of the church in Smyrna, "'I know your tribulation
and your poverty (but you are rich)" (Rev. 2:9).

No health and welfare successes here, but there were spiritual
riches of God's grace everywhere amidst this poverty. Spiritual
riches in the midst of economic poverty – that is the pattern
with a few exceptions among early disciples of Christ. Christ
promises us spiritual riches, his grace. And yes, that grace is
sufficient for us!

Questions for reflection

1. What are some images that come to your mind when you think of tremendous pain? You may not want to discuss them.

2. What are some examples you can give of friends who show tremendous spiritual strength in the midst of severe physical deformities or illness?

3. What do you think was Paul's thorn in the flesh? Why doesn't it matter so much to know specifically what it was?

4. Read 2 Corinthians 8:9, 14. God's grace in these verses is seen through the actions of the Macedonians. How can God's great grace be seen today through the actions of believers?

5. Why do we so often want to see physical blessings when God is promising spiritual blessings?

6. What are some examples that come to your mind of poor Christians who are actually rich spiritually?

Chapter 12

" My Power Is Made Perfect in Weakness "

"For When I am Weak, then I am strong" (2 Cor. 12:10).

Text: 2 Corinthians 12:1-10 again

The spiritual successes of the apostle Paul are staggering. A survey of selected history professors even rated him ahead of Jesus in his influence on the world.[42] The professors gloss over the fact that with no Jesus there was no Paul. However, without doubt he was the key figure in the spreading of Christianity throughout the Roman Empire in the first century. He wrote 13 of the 27 books of the New Testament.

With so many spiritual successes, Paul was a ripe candidate for pride, success's constant companion. Then came the thorn, the painful thorn (2 Cor. 12:7-10). Though Paul called it a messenger of Satan, God allowed it. Why? Paul knew – "to keep me from becoming conceited" (vs. 8).

So often we cry out in the midst of our pain, "why?" and the answer is often the same as that given to Paul—to keep us from becoming conceited. There are blessings in the pain!

The blessing in the pain helped Paul to rejoice even with his thorn!

> Therefore I will boast all the more gladly of my weaknesses, so that the power of Christ may rest upon me. For the sake of Christ, then, I am content with weaknesses, insults, hardships, persecutions, and calamities. For when I am weak, then I am strong. (vss. 9b, 10)

The same thing happens to disciples today. When do we pray most fervently? When do we think most of eternity with God? When groaning with all sorts of thorns! When we are weak, we are strong!

Examples of Friends

Seeing Billy Crafts for the first time was a rather shocking experience for a carefree 11 year old. As I watched him lying in his portable bed at the front of the church building, I could see that he was completely paralyzed except for his arms and facial muscles. He was unable even to move his head to look at those who talked with him. It was depressing to wonder what kind of life a person imprisoned in such a body could have and my first impulse was to get away from such a distressing sight.

In spite of my initial fear of Billy, something drew me to
him. His hearty laughter as he joked with the group of people
gathered around his cot after services indicated that the owner
of the wretched body was a happy man who enjoyed life in
spite of the painful rheumatoid arthritis that had crippled him.
More than anything else, my timidity about Billy was replaced
with curiosity when someone told me that he was a ham radio
operator. I began to shyly approach Billy's portable bed after
church services to see if I could overhear anything about this
amazing ham radio business. Before I knew it, he noticed me and
asked me to come on over to talk. He began talking to me about
his hobby, answering my shy questions with a reassuring smile.

Billy eventually became my best adult friend, teaching me the
Morse code and helping me get my ham radio license, which
I still have (W2NL). We spent countless hours together both
in person and on the airways.

Billy was often sick because his paralyzed body could not fight
off infection well. However, life seems eternal to teenagers, and
I took it for granted that he would always get well. I should
have known that his fragile body couldn't last forever. When
Jimmy, Billy's brother, interrupted my P.E. class one morning
to tell me that Billy had died, I could hardly believe him at first.
As the truth dawned on me, I felt numbed. I tried in vain to
hide my tears from my teenage companions in the gym.

Perhaps the most important lesson that Billy taught me was
that life can be meaningful and even happy in spite of pain
and deformities.

A rather embittered man once asked me how a loving God could allow children to go through life with serious deformities. At first, I sputtered around about not understanding many things about this world, but then I began to think about Billy and the more I thought of him. the more confidence I gained in answering the question. I told the gentleman about him. Would it have been better for him not to have lived? Was Billy a proof that there is no such thing as a loving compassionate God? Instead of providing a reason to doubt, Billy's life gave testimony to the power of God to give hope and meaning even to one with a severely crippled body. Perhaps Billy's agonizing thorn deepened his character. Perhaps because of it he had a better understanding of the empty promises of this world and clearer vision of heaven. I believe that Billy was so strong because he was so weak!

I knew David Hartsell in college as a playful and fun loving baseball player who quickly drew others to him. After graduating, he preached among churches, primarily in Alabama, for a number of years, becoming quite popular with his quick wit and positive outlook.

Then disaster struck. Doctors discovered a tumor in David's brain and after a serious operation he gradually began to recover and even began to preach again. But he was a different man. Someone told me, "David's preaching is much deeper, has much more substance and is more profitable than before." What happened? When David became weak, then he became strong.

However, David's tumor came back. Complications from a second operation have left him unable to preach and robbed him of his mental sharpness. And yet, he still has a smile and a positive outlook for all who come to see him. Perhaps his family struggles with this thorn more than he does. However, with David and his family there are no illusions about the shallow attractions of this world. They long to go where there are no tears, no tumors and no pain.

A Personal Example

It's disconcerting to see nurses whispering among themselves as they look at your heart monitor! That happened to me when going through a routine colonoscopy.

Finally the doctor came and said, "You must see a heart specialist."

"What's wrong?" I asked.

"You have an abnormal heart rhythm."

As soon as the cardiologist saw my EKG he said, "You have something called a left bundle branch block that often indicates a serious heart problems. We're going to have to do some tests on your heart."

The day after a stress test, while eating pancakes with my parents at a restaurant in Budd Lake, New Jersey, the doctor called on my cell phone and said. "We believe that you have had two heart attacks which have damaged your heart. Are you having any pains in your chest?"

I was starting to have them!

"Perhaps some slight pain," I told him.

The pains seemed to grow and the doctor decided to admit me to the hospital until he could arrange for me to have cardiac catheterization where a tube would be inserted from my groin into the heart to determine the amount of damage.

While waiting that night in the hospital for the test the next day, I thought a lot about God, the temporary nature of life and especially my family. What would happen to them if my heart had been so badly damaged that I had only a short time to live? I prayed more fervently than usual.

After a while a nurse suggested I watch TV. There was an NFL game on which I usually enjoy, but I felt rather detached as I watched. "What importance does it really have?" I thought. During one of the countless interruptions that always accompany a football game, there was a clever commercial for Toyota. I've always liked Toyotas and own one now, but in watching the commercial I thought, "If I'm about to die, what do I need with a Toyota?"

The next morning, I was transported by ambulance (a $4500 ride!) to another hospital where the cardiologist inserted the tube into my heart as I watched his progress on the monitor trying to decipher the meaning of it all. He injected a little dye, looked briefly at the monitor and exclaimed, "Your heart's fine! There's no sign of heart disease!"

"Then why did you scare me to death?" I asked.

The experience was somewhat traumatizing and yet the relatively minor scars that came from it were good scars, scars that helped me put life into perspective. During the days after the scare, I prayed to God to help me to maintain the perspectives that I had when I thought death might be near: life is short, my body is weak and decaying, football and other aspects of the entertainment world must be kept in perspective, etc. How well have I maintained those life assessments? Not perfectly. I sometimes find myself caught up again with too much stress about things that don't really matter that much, but I don't think it happens now as much as before. It's good for me to go back and revisit that scare. When I was weak, then I was strong. I need my little scars from that time to remind me of that!

For many however, the dreaded doctor's call to the office after a test is not a false alarm. The malignancy is real, the heart disease is life threating, time is short. That real alarm will probably come for me some day, perhaps not so far into the future. Then I hope I can remind myself of Billy Crafts, David Hartsell and dozens of others like them who have blessed my life, so that I can remind myself that when I'm weak, I'm strong.

Dreams Interrupted by Reality

I love to talk to Christian teenagers about their dreams. Some believe that with God's help they can lay out a nice, clean plan for their future lives. Sometimes my conversations with them go something like this:

Me – "What do you plan to do during the next ten years?"

Them –

> I'm just about out of high school now and plan to go to this respected university and I've even been able to get a nice scholarship. You know that growing companies are increasingly seeking out graduates in my field of study and I'm confident I can get a good job.

> Then, I hope to marry a good Christian and have a nice family. We could buy a little house with a white fence and have three or four kids and a nice dog, maybe a Labrador retriever.

> I'm going to work hard with my spouse to raise up children that like to read and study the Bible. I hope they like sports, but not too much, like good music and literature, but not too much and will always seek our advice as parents and do what's right.

As I listen, I smile since I enjoy their optimism. It's fine for them to have it, especially when they want to serve God in their future lives. However, I know that reality usually has a way of getting into the way of such idealism.

Those respected universities sometimes have tough classes. There is such a thing as chemistry! There are bitter and sarcastic professors who seem to take glee in destroying faith in the name of promoting thought. Then, when leaving school at whatever stage, with or without a degree, those good jobs often aren't easy to obtain.

When the time comes to seek a spouse, they find imperfection! Young men are often damaged by pornography and young women are twisted by shallow materialistic expectations. A growing number of single young Christians would like to get married but have difficulty finding someone compatible. When they reach their 30's and 40's they begin to see their dreams of three kids and a dog fading.

Often when marriage is possible, the challenges of molding two different lives with two different temperaments into one can become overwhelming. "No one told me it was going to be this difficult!"

And then come the kids! They have minds of their own and don't want to cooperate. How much should we discipline them? When should we apply the rod of discipline (Prov. 14:34) and when should we be patient? Why are they so rebellious?

We think child rearing is challenging when they are small, but we don't know what challenging is until they become teenagers. They begin to struggle with their own deformities, wounds and scars - physical, spiritual and emotional. Sometimes the wounds are deep! How we want to help them! However, they often don't want our help or if they do, they don't want to show us that they want it.

In the midst of all the turmoil, pain, conflict and wounds of every kind, we cry out, "God fix all of this!"

And his reply?

"My grace is sufficient for you, for my power is made perfect in weakness."

That must be the mantra of our often-imperfect lives – "My grace is sufficient for you."

Instead of sinking into despair when life isn't perfect, may God help us to remind ourselves that his overwhelming, overpowering and abundant grace is sufficient for all of our needs. That grace is what we must seek and treasure above all else. If we do, our painful wounds can turn into teaching scars that give us wisdom and perspective.

The true way of Christ isn't the way of prosperity or instant physical healing. It is the way of joy in the midst of pain, hope in the midst of anguish and purpose in the midst of despair. May God help us to see that fact through our scars and trust it!

Questions for reflection – Read 2 Corinthians 12:7-10 again

1. Can you recall a time in your own life when pride attacked you after you felt you had enjoyed some spiritual success?

2. How can God use "messengers of Satan" such as Paul's thorn, to teach us spiritual lessons? Should we blame God or Satan when we suffer? How can we cooperate with God to turn painful "messengers of Satan" into positive spiritual lessons?

3. We sometimes go through periods where we seek God more fervently. When has there been such a time in your life? Was that time associated with a particular trial you were going through?

4. Write down as many applications for your life as you can from the verses about Paul's thorn in the flesh, 1 Corinthians 12:7-10. How can it help us have a proper perspective about suffering?

5. Have you been tempted to try to read a wealth-oriented message into a spiritual book, the Bible? What are some verses and Biblical concepts that can provide spiritual medicine for that misconception?

Chapter 13

Don't Forget The Scars!

"One thing I do know, that though I was blind, now I see" (John 9:25).

Texts: Matthew 19:7-9; John 9:1-7; 24-34

I'm sad today. A young man who I knew a number of years ago as a zealous young disciple wrote a Facebook post stating that he no longer believes in the bodily resurrection of Jesus. When pressed a little, he stated that he didn't think that Luke wrote Acts. When pressed even more he stated that he thought the apostles were sincere in the testimony about Jesus but that "cultural assumptions led them to misinterpret the significance of what they saw."

Why does my friend reject the testimony of the apostles by implying that they misunderstood what they saw? When talking with mutual friends about my concern for him, I found out that in the past dozen or so years, he has become known for seeking questions rather than answers. To make matters worse, he has become fascinated with worldly scholarship and has tended to seek his questions not from truth seekers but in the world of skeptical academia.

When asked for specific reasons for his loss of faith, he mentioned some differing details in the post resurrection accounts, in particular Matthew's account that Jesus would see the apostles in Galilee (28:7, 16) while saying nothing about his appearances to them in Jerusalem (Luke 22:36-48; John 20:19-29).

My friend and others like him forget that though there are different details in the four gospels, it is not a matter of either/or, but rather both/and. Jesus appeared to his disciples both in Judea (Luke, John) and in Galilee (Matthew, Mark, John). Matthew and Mark emphasized his Galilean appearances, Luke, his appearances in Judea and John, both. There is no real contradiction here or anywhere else as numerous Biblical scholars have pointed out through the centuries, but some seek questions rather than answers.

Another young adult I know states his problem with the treatment of women under the Law of Moses. Why could they be divorced but they had no right to divorce their husbands? Why were other practices that demean women such as bigamy and polygamy tolerated? Jesus gave the answer in Matthew 19:8, at least in part, when speaking of divorce. Such practices were tolerated (not promoted) because of the hardness of heart of the primitive Jews who lived a millennium and a half before Jesus. The primitive cultures of the time were violent and did not treat women as equals. The purpose of the law of Moses was never meant to reflect God's ideals regarding marriage or social relationships but rather to take primitive, hard-hearted people incrementally from where they were towards the point where in Christ they would be capable of returning to God's ideals that he stated from the beginning in texts like Genesis 2:24-26. Other passages which point out this purpose of the law of Moses, to prepare primitive people for God's ideal, are Galatians 3:23-25 and Hebrews 8:8-13. However, the problem is that some seek questions rather than answers!

Yes, it is sometimes necessary to direct ourselves to specific issues to help our friends as they struggle with their faith. However, there is danger in becoming entangled in minute details of their complaints to the point that we overlook their fundamental problem. Rarely is it simple confusion about some issue like harmonizing different biblical accounts, but rather that they are forgetting the obvious— the scars. What about those thousands of scars on the backs of the apostles and other witnesses? Did they willingly receive them for something so fuzzy, so indefinite that they misinterpreted the significance of what they saw? Were they willing to die for something so vague? Why overlook the overwhelming truth revealed in the obvious answers to these questions because of a fixation on details that are superfluous in comparison?

Impossible to Explain Christianity without the Scars

A powerful force shook the Roman Empire in the first century. It wasn't a swarming military power like Islam or a dominant economic philosophy like Marxism. What rattled the foundations of the Roman world was the testimony of unsophisticated witnesses who were utterly determined to go through appalling privation to proclaim their message— that they saw a dead man who proclaimed a life-changing message come back to life. The witnesses had no academic or social status to give them credibility. It was the sheer audacity of their testimony and the thousands of collective scars that backed it up that made them so compelling. Their message turned the Roman world upside down in spite of the fact that almost every other factor seemed to work against them.

A classic commentator on the New Testament from the 18th century, James MacKnight, said regarding the force of their testimony, "the greatness of this power can only be estimated by the greatness of the obstacles which it had to remove, and by the greatness of the effects which it then produced."[43]

He then went on to point out that the apostles' message had a significant effect as soon as it touched any corner of the globe, changing confused and sensual pagans into serious, holy people—this in spite status quo's political influence, traditions and academic elitism.

He concluded, "the ties of blood and friendship were to be broken, considerations of ease and interest were to be silenced; nay, the love of life itself was to be cast out; all which were obstacles to the heathen changing their faith and practice, next to insurmountable."

That's a good quote even after over two hundred years. The scars were powerful! They are the only logical explanation for the explosion of Christianity in the first century.

It is easy in the 21st century to become infatuated with human scholarship and philosophy and then become confused by it. When that happens, we begin to think that we should be able to understand every intellectual challenge that theologians can invent. Frustrated and overwhelmed by the avalanche of "what ifs" and other details we were never designed to understand, we find ourselves forgetting the power of the simple message that changed the world. Then we drift into the self-absorbed meaningless existence that is becoming so common in our world. A refocus on the testimony of those scarred witnesses, and the fact that they had absolutely no doubts or reservations - none! zilch! zippo!- can put our doubts in their place and allow the message they revealed to powerfully mold our lives like it did theirs.

Consequences of Rejecting the Scars

The testimony of the scars has benefited Western Culture with an advanced system of ethics that in turn has given us many advantages in spite of the fact that it has been followed so poorly. The increased distancing from the testimony of the scars and their accompanying moral beliefs has led to less order. Two ghastly world wars and hundreds of millions of victims of atheist monsters like Stalin, Mao, Pol Pot and others should have served as a wakeup call; but most unbelievers pay no attention. They believe they can blithely reject the scars and concept of a loving yet judging God, with no ill effects. Thus, Paul's description of the pagan world of the first century increasingly describes our own Western Civilization—

> ...filled with all manner of unrighteousness, evil, covetousness, malice... envy, murder, strife, deceit, maliciousness. They are gossips, slanderers, haters of God, insolent, haughty, boastful, inventors of evil, disobedient to parents, foolish, faithless, heartless, ruthless... (Romans 1:29-31)

Unbelief is just as powerless to help confused individuals as it is cultures. John Ortberg put it this way,

> I have never heard anybody say, "One day I realized there was no God, no one behind reality, no life after death. I realized existence is a meaningless accident, begun by chance and destined for oblivion, and it changed my life. I used to be addicted to alcohol, but now the law of natural selection has set me free. I used to be greedy, but now the story of the Big Bang has made me generous. I used to be afraid, but now random chance has made me brave."[44]

To reject the testimony of the scars is to reject the order that it has tried to give us, it is to reject the clearest standard of right and wrong the world has ever known along with the balancing concepts of mercy and grace. The short-term consequences are painful; the long-term consequences appalling.

What We Can and Cannot Understand

We routinely receive truths on the basis of what we can understand while also accepting that there is much we can't grasp. This is a principle we accept in all areas of our lives.

In the realm of science, we don't understand much about how genetics work. *Scientific American* bluntly states – "We do not know what most of our DNA does, nor how, or to what extent it governs traits." It even admits, "The very definition of 'gene' is hotly debated."[45]

Though we don't know much about how DNA works, that doesn't keep us from accepting that fact that it exists.

As mentioned earlier, my wife, Beverly, suffers from lupus, but we are thankful she has had an outstanding rheumatologist, Harry Spiera, from Mt. Sinai Hospital in New York City. He is a brilliant pioneer in lupus research and treatment and has helped Beverly with a mix of various drugs. He believes that Plaquenil, a drug designed to combat malaria, has been the most effective in keeping her lupus at bay.

"How does Plaquenil work?" I asked him.

"We're not really sure," he responded. "It just seems to work for a number of lupus patients."

So, we understand that Plaquenil works in marvelous ways for some lupus patients. There is much we don't understand about it, but we gladly accept it anyway.

To reject transforming and enlightening truths because there are relatively unimportant details that we don't understand is irrational!

The Blind Man in John 9

Here are two facts from John chapter 9:

(1) Jesus healed a man who was born blind. His parents and dozens of neighbors confirmed that he had been blind from birth.

(2) Jesus healed him on the Jewish Sabbath.

Which of these two facts carried more weight with the Jewish leaders? The second! They overlooked the obvious "elephant in the room" because they got hung up over a relatively unimportant detail—that it happened on the Sabbath. Rather than re-evaluating their presuppositions about Sabbath regulations, they clung tenaciously to them while ignoring the obvious.

The blind man wasn't going to make that mistake after he had been healed. When the religious leaders confronted him with their Sabbath day hang-ups and called Jesus a sinner because he violated them, the blind man responded simply, "Whether he is a sinner I do not know. One thing I do know, that though I was blind, now I see" (John 9:25). In other words, "I'm not sure about that" (whether Jesus violated Sabbath regulations), "but I am sure about this!" (I was blind and now I see!)

When my friends begin to focus so much on little details they don't understand that they ignore overwhelming and transforming truths, the witnesses cry out against them, "What about the scars?"

- "Why didn't Matthew mention the post resurrection appearances in Judea?"

The blind man's answer would be – "I'm not sure about every aspect of harmonizing the four gospels, but what about the scars?"

- Why did God tolerate men divorcing their wives under Jewish law but not vice-versa?"

The blind man's answer would be - "I don't know the hows and whys of every aspect of the law of Moses, but what about the scars?"

For every difficult detail in the Bible that someone wants to gives as reason for not believing, he must face an even more troubling question in his unbelief—What about the scars? Every time we start to doubt when contemplating the suffering in the world, the vastness of the universe, the invisibility of God and dozens of other doubt producers, those bloodied and scarred witnesses call us back to reality— "What about my scars?"

Before man can truly face who he is and what his future might be, he must face the 2,000-year old question—What about those scars? Do they reflect a mindless masochism by hundreds of witnesses who really had no idea of what they saw? Or, do they reflect determined testimony of those who knew exactly what they saw - an earth-shattering miracle that backs up a life-changing message from a loving Creator? That is the question we must all answer! The way we respond to the scars may determine whether we see the marvel of life as the results of chains of millions of genetic accidents or as the product of a master Creator. Beyond that, our response determines whether we see that Creator as a mysterious and distant force or one interested deeply in human affairs and in our personal lives. Our response to their scars and especially to his scars, will determine if we have any practical way of turning our own gruesome wounds into healing scars. Finally, the consequences of our response to the message of the scars will determine what kind of life we have in an overwhelmingly negative or positive way. More importantly, our reaction to the scars will determine our eternal fate.

Perhaps the most critical issue facing our lives is— Will we ignore the collective scars? Or will we ask the questions about the scars with gritty determination; seeking answers and healing that can only come from the great Physician?

Final questions for reflection

1. Do you have any friends who have lost their faith? What reasons do they give? What are they overlooking?

2. Have you sometimes allowed yourself to become so distracted by relatively unimportant questions that you overlook overwhelming truths? Why do we do that? Why is it foolish?

3. Why do you think that those who reject Christ and the testimony of the scars overlook the consequences of doing that? What are some consequences that your friends who have rejected Christ have had to suffer? How has our country and Western Culture suffered from rejecting some of the fundamental concepts of living taught by Jesus Christ?

4. Can you think of any examples that illustrate the fact that we believe on the basis of what we understand while accepting the fact that there are some details we do not understand?

5. How has your consideration of the scars of Christ and His apostles and witnesses strengthened your faith and purpose in life? How can you help spread the message of the scars?

End Notes

1 Walt Guthrie, http://waltguthrieswretchedexcesses.blogspot.com/2011/06/anthony-wiener-and-charles-woods.html, November21, 2014.

2 http://en.wikipedia.org/wiki/Charles_Woods, November 21 2014.

3 http://www.iprospero.com/shpusa/books/chapters/Murray3-17.pdf, November 21, 2014.

4 Jalynn Olsen Padilla, *Army of "Cripples": Northern Civil War Amputees, Disability, and Manhood in Victorian America*, Dissertation submitted to the Faculty of the University of Delaware, https://books.google.com/books/about/Army_of_cripples.html?id=I_z5ngEACAAJNovember 11, 2015 p.3.

5 Vance Havner, http://www.essenceofworship.org/suffering/432-suffering2, 10/20/2015.

6 Adam Clarke, *Commentary on 2 Corinthians*, http://www.studylight.org/commentaries/acc/view.cgi?bk=46&ch=11, November 24, 2014.

7 Albert Barnes, *Commentary on 2nd Corinthians*, http://www.studylight.org/commentaries/bnb/view.cgi?bk=46&ch=11, November 24, 2014.

8 Brian Rapske, *The Book of Acts and Paul in Roman Custody*, Grand Rapids, Michigan, William B. Eerdmans Publishing, 1994 p. 124.

9 http://www.boston-catholic-journal.com/tortures-and-torments-of-the-christian-martyrs-de-ss-martyrum-cruciatibus-gallonio/tortures-and-torments-of-the-christian-martyrs-chapter-4.htm, December 14, 2015.

10 Brian Rapske.

11 J.W. McGarvey, *New Commentary on Acts of the Apostles*, Cincinnati, Ohio, The Standard Publishing Foundation, no copyright date given, p. 101.

12 Alex Lickerman M.D., "Why We Lie," <http://www.psychologytoday.com/blog/happiness-in-world/201003/why-we-lie> December 30, 2014.

13 Quoted by Sean McDowell, http://magazine.biola.edu/article/13-fall/did-the-apostles-really-die-as-martyrs-for-their-f/ December 30, 2014.

14 Edward F. Marquart, "Sermons from Seattle" http://www.sermonsfromseattle.com/series_b_the_passion_story_GA_p4.htm, March 3, 2016.

15 David McClister, "The Scourging of Jesus," Truth Magazine, Vol. XLIV: 1 p 11,12 January 2000. http://www.truthmagazine.com/archives/volume44/v440106010.htm, March 3, 2016.

16 Eusebius, *Ecclesiastical History*, Book 4, chap. 15.

17 William D. Edwards, MD; Wesley J. Gabel, MDiv; Floyd E. Hosmer, MS, AMI, Study of the Physical Death of Jesus, http://www.frugalsites.net/jesus/crucifixion.htm, November 19, 2016.

18 Vassilios Tzaferis, Crucifixion—The Archaeological Evidence, http://www.biblicalarchaeology.org/daily/biblical-topics/crucifixion/a-tomb-in-jerusalem-reveals-the-history-of-crucifixion-and-roman-crucifixion-methods/, December 13, 2015..

19 Edwards, Gabel and Hosmer.

20 http://www.thepathoftruth.com/the-issues-of-life/the-false-and-misleading-gospel-of-accepting-jesus-christ.htm. December 3, 2015.

21 Michael Shank, *Muscle and a Shovel,* self-published, 4th edition revised September 2013, p. 108.

22 Shank

23 Alfred Plummer, *1 John,* The Pulpit Commentary, London, England, Anson D.F. Radolph and Company, page 2.

24 Todd Deatherage, "What to Do About Angry Christianity? http?//www.relevantmagazine.com/life/what-do-about-angry-christianity, November 26, 2015."

25 John McArthur, *The Power of Suffering, Strengthening Your Faith in the Refiner's Fire,* Kindle Edition, Location 1306.

26 Rape, Abuse and Incest National Network, https://rainn.org/get-information/statistics/sexual-assault-victims, November 20, 2015.

27 Rape, Abuse and Incest National Network.

28 Alanna Vagianos , http://www.huffingtonpost.com/2015/02/19/1-in-3-women-sexually-harassed-work-cosmopolitan_n_6713814.html, November 30, 2015.

29 Carolyn Coker Ross, M.D. , "Why do Women Hate Their Bodies?" "http://www.discoverthenetworks.org/viewSubCategory.asp?id=367, December 4, 2015.

30 Mary A. Kassians with Dale McCleskey, *In My Father's House: Finding Your Heart's True Home,* Broadman and Holman Publishers, Nashville, Tennessee, 2005, p. 4.

31 http://psychcentral.com/blog/archives/2012/06/02/why-do-women-hate-their-bodies/, December 4, 2015.

32 Coker Ross.

33 Dr. Andra Brosh, "The 5 Stages of Emotional Triage for the Divorced, Betrayed, Broken-Hearted, and Discarded" http://www.huffingtonpost.com/dr-andra-brosh-/the-5-stages-of-emotional_b_3430054.html, December 8, 2015.

34 Serena DeGarmo, http://awordywoman.com/how-not-to-teach-your-girls-about-purity/ October 29, 2015.

35 Ashely Conzelmann, Marissa Hernandez, Tenzing Sherpa, "Euphemisms for Death,http://www.lvc.edu/rel314/euph.aspx, December 9, 2015.

36 Chris Raymond, "101 Euphemisms for Dead, Death or Dying," http://dying.about.com/od/Funeral_Memorial_Planning/a/101-Euphemisms-For-Dead-Death-Or-Dying.htm, December 9, 2015.

37 Cliff Vaughn, "Ted Turner Talks About His Faith," http://www.ethicsdaily.com/ted-turner-talks-about-his-faith-cms-2247#sthash.GE5tybHIb.dpuf, December 9, 2015.

38 Bertrand Russell, "A Free Man's Worship," Mysticism and Logic and Other Essays, London, George Allen & Unwin Ltd. 1938, p 47,48, Quoted by Batsell Barrett Baxter, I Believe Because, Baker Book House, Grand Rapids, Michigan, 1971, p.78.

39 Sir William M. Ramsey, St. Paul the Traveler and the Roman Citizen http://www.ccel.org/ccel/ramsay/paul_roman.viii.html?highlight=thorn,malaria#highlight.

40 Karl Kautsky, Foundations Of Christianity (Orabis & Windrush, 1973 ed)., pp. 9,323.

41 http://www.aletheiacollege.net/bl/16-3-3Rich_And_Poor_In_The_First_Century.htm#n1, November 9, 2015.

42 David M. Rhoads, The Challenge of Diversity: The Witness of Paul and the Gospels, Augsburg Fortress, Minneapolis, Minnesota, 1996 p. 56.

43 James MacKnight, A New Literal Translation from the Original Greek of all the Apostolic Epistles with a Commentary and Notes. Grand Rapids, Michigan, Baker Book House, 1949, p. 222 (Comment on 2 Cor. 4:7).

44 John Ortberg, Faith and Doubt, Grand Rapids, Michigan, Zondervan Publishing, 2008, p. 167.

45 Phillip Ball Nature Magazine, http://www.scientificamerican.com/article/dna-at-60-still-much-to-learn/ 8/3/2015.

Also from Mount Bethel Publishing,

"Foy Short, A Life in Southern Africa"

Biography of Foy Short, a pioneer evangelist who lived in what is now Zambia and
Zimbabwe from 1922 through 1995. The
book explores not only the traditional hazards
he faced as an African "missionary" (wild
animals, primitive tribesmen and dangerous
travel) but also the doctrinal and spiritual
challenges that he and his family had to battle
in establishing congregations and training
African evangelists.

by Gardner Hall, 244 pages

Convictions Versus Mercy

Conviction or Mercy? Which characteristic
should most exemplify those who want
to follow Christ? Many Christians tend to
emphasize one or the other but not both.
This book emphasizes the importance of
merging the two to be truly like Christ.
Though combining mercy and conviction has
always been a challenge throughout history,
it is especially difficult now as our culture
is increasingly affected by a Postmodern
worldview and the backlash against it.

by Gardner Hall, 144 pages

"Familias edificadas sobre la roca"

A study of God's family in the Spanish language.

All Available in Kindle and Paperback formats
Order from Amazon.com or your favorite bookstore

Made in the USA
Columbia, SC
07 June 2017